FREE Test Taking Tips DVD Offer

To help us better serve you, we have developed a Test Taking Tips DVD that we would like to give you for FREE. **This DVD covers world-class test taking tips that you can use to be even more successful when you are taking your test.**

All that we ask is that you email us your feedback about your study guide. Please let us know what you thought about it – whether that is good, bad or indifferent.

To get your **FREE Test Taking Tips DVD**, email freedvd@studyguideteam.com with "FREE Test Taking Tips DVD" in the subject line and the following information in the body of the email:

    a. The title of your study guide.

    b. Your product rating on a scale of 1-5, with 5 being the highest rating.

    c. Your feedback about the study guide. What did you think of it?

    d. Your full name and shipping address to send your free DVD.

If you have any questions or concerns, please don't hesitate to contact us at freedvd@studyguideteam.com.

Thanks again!

Corrections Officer
Exam Study Guide

Table of Contents

Quick Overview

As you draw closer to taking your exam, preparing becomes more and more important. Thankfully, you have this study guide to help you get ready. Use this guide to help keep your studying on track and refer to it often.

This study guide contains several key sections that will help you be successful on your exam. The guide contains tips for what you should do the night before and the day of the test. Also included are test-taking tips. Knowing the right information is not always enough. Many well-prepared test takers struggle with exams. These tips will help equip you to accurately read, assess, and answer test questions.

A large part of the guide is devoted to showing you what content to expect on the exam and to helping you better understand that content. Near the end of this guide is a practice test so that you can see how well you have grasped the content. Then, answers explanations are provided so that you can understand why you missed certain questions.

Don't try to cram the night before you take your exam. This is not a wise strategy for a few reasons. First, your retention of the information will be low. Your time would be better used by reviewing information you already know rather than trying to learn lots of new information. Second, you will likely become stressed as you try to gain large amount of knowledge in a short amount of time. Third, you will be depriving yourself of sleep. So be sure to go to bed at a reasonable time the night before. Being well-rested helps you focus and remain calm.

Be sure to eat a substantial breakfast the morning of the exam. If you are taking the exam in the afternoon, be sure to have a good lunch as well. Being hungry is distracting and can make it difficult to focus. You have hopefully spent lots of time preparing for the exam. Don't let an empty stomach get in the way of success!

When travelling to the testing center, leave earlier than needed. That way, you have a buffer in case you experience any delays. This will help you remain calm and will keep you from missing your appointment time at the testing center.

Be sure to pace yourself during the exam. Don't try to rush through the exam. There is no need to risk performing poorly on the exam just so you can leave the testing center early. Allow yourself to use all of the allotted time if needed.

Remain positive while taking the exam even if you feel like you are performing poorly. Thinking about the content you should have mastered will not help you perform better on the exam.

Once the exam is complete, take some time to relax. Even if you feel that you need to take the exam again, you will be well served by some down time before you begin studying again. It's often easier to convince yourself to study if you know that it will come with a reward!

Test-Taking Strategies

1. Predicting the Answer

When you feel confident in your preparation for a multiple-choice test, try predicting the answer before reading the answer choices. This is especially useful on questions that test objective factual knowledge or that ask you to fill in a blank. By predicting the answer before reading the available choices, you eliminate the possibility that you will be distracted or led astray by an incorrect answer choice. You will feel much more confident in your selection if you read the question, predict the answer, and then find your prediction among the answer choices. After using this strategy, be sure to still read all of the answer choices carefully and completely. If you feel unprepared, you should not attempt to predict the answers. This would be a waste of time and an opportunity for your mind to wander in the wrong direction.

2. Reading the Whole Question

Too often, test takers scan a multiple-choice question, recognize a few familiar words, and immediately jump to the answer choices. Test authors are aware of this common impatience, and they will sometimes prey upon it. For instance, a test author might subtly turn the question into a negative, or he or she might redirect the focus of the question right at the end. The only way to avoid falling into these traps is to read the entirety of the question carefully before reading the answer choices.

3. Looking for Wrong Answers

Long and complicated multiple-choice questions can be intimidating. One way to simplify a difficult multiple-choice question is to eliminate all of the answer choices that are clearly wrong. In most sets of answers, there will be at least one selection that can be dismissed right away. If the test is administered on paper, the test taker could draw a line through it to indicate that it may be ignored; otherwise, the test taker will have to perform this operation mentally or on scratch paper. In either case, once the obviously incorrect answers have been eliminated, the remaining choices may be considered. Sometimes identifying the clearly wrong answers will give the test taker some information about the correct answer. For instance, if one of the remaining answer choices is a direct opposite of one of the eliminated answer choices, it may well be the correct answer. The opposite of obviously wrong is obviously right! Of course, this is not always the case. Some answers are obviously incorrect simply because they are irrelevant to the question being asked. Still, identifying and eliminating some incorrect answer choices is a good way to simplify a multiple-choice question.

4. Don't Overanalyze

Anxious test takers often overanalyze questions. When you are nervous, your brain will often run wild causing you to make associations and discover clues that don't actually exist. If you feel that this may be a problem for you, do whatever you can to slow down during the test. Try taking a deep breath or counting to ten. As you read and consider the question, restrict yourself to the particular words used by the author. Avoid thought tangents about what the author *really* meant, or what he or she was *trying* to say. The only things that matter on a multiple-choice test are the words that are actually in the question. You must avoid reading too much into a multiple-choice question, or supposing that the writer meant something other than what he or she wrote.

5. No Need for Panic

It is wise to learn as many strategies as possible before taking a multiple-choice test, but it is likely that you will come across a few questions for which you simply don't know the answer. In this situation, avoid panicking. Because most multiple-choice tests include dozens of questions, the relative value of a single wrong answer is small. Moreover, your failure on one question has no effect on your success elsewhere on the test. As much as possible, you should compartmentalize each question on a multiple-choice test. In other words, you should not allow your feelings about one question to affect your success on the others. When you find a question that you either don't understand or don't know how to answer, just take a deep breath and do your best. Read the entire question slowly and carefully. Try rephrasing the question a couple of different ways. Then, read all of the answer choices carefully. After eliminating obviously wrong answers, make a selection and move on to the next question.

6. Confusing Answer Choices

When working on a difficult multiple-choice question, there may be a tendency to focus on the answer choices that are the easiest to understand. Many people, whether consciously or not, gravitate to the answer choices that require the least concentration, knowledge, and memory. This is a mistake. When you come across an answer choice that is confusing, you need to give it extra attention. A question might be confusing because you do not know the subject matter to which it refers. If this is the case, don't eliminate the answer before you have affirmatively settled on another. When you come across an answer choice of this type, set it aside as you look at the remaining choices. If you can confidently assert that one of the other choices is correct, you can leave the confusing answer aside. Otherwise, you will need to take a moment to try to better understand the confusing answer choice. Rephrasing is one way to tease out the sense of a confusing answer choice.

7. Your First Instinct

Many people struggle with multiple-choice tests because they overthink the questions. If you have studied sufficiently for the test, you should be prepared to trust your first instinct once you have carefully and completely read the question and all of the answer choices. There is a great deal of research to suggest that the mind can come to the correct conclusion very quickly once it has obtained all of the relevant information. At times, it may seem to you as if your intuition is working faster even than your reasoning mind. This may in fact be true. The knowledge you obtain while studying may be retrieved from your subconscious before you have a chance to work out the associations that support it. Verify your instinct by working out the reasons that it should be trusted.

8. Key Words

Many test takers struggle with multiple-choice questions because they have poor reading comprehension skills. Quickly reading and understanding a multiple-choice question requires a mixture of skill and experience. To help with this, try jotting down a few key words and phrases on a piece of scrap paper. Doing this concentrates the process of reading and forces the mind to weigh the relative importance of the question's parts. In selecting words and phrases to write down, the test taker thinks about the question more deeply and carefully. This is especially true for multiple-choice questions that are preceded by a long prompt.

9. Subtle Negatives

One of the oldest tricks in the multiple-choice test writer's book is to subtly reverse the meaning of a question with a word like *not* or *except*. If you are not paying attention to each word in the question, you can easily be led astray by this trick. For instance, a common question format is, "Which of the following is...?" Obviously, if the question instead is, "Which of the following is not....?," then the answer will be quite different. Even worse, the test makers are aware of the potential for this mistake and will include one answer choice that would be correct if the question were not negated or reversed. A test taker who misses the reversal will find what he or she believes to be a correct answer and will be so confident that he or she will fail to reread the question and discover the original error. The only way to avoid this is to practice a wide variety of multiple-choice questions and to pay close attention to each and every word.

10. Reading Every Answer Choice

It may seem obvious, but you should always read every one of the answer choices! Too many test takers fall into the habit of scanning the question and assuming that they understand the question because they recognize a few key words. From there, they pick the first answer choice that answers the question they believe they have read. Test takers who read all of the answer choices might discover that one of the latter answer choices is actually *more* correct. Moreover, reading all of the answer choices can remind you of facts related to the question that can help you arrive at the correct answer. Sometimes, a misstatement or incorrect detail in one of the latter answer choices will trigger your memory of the subject and will enable you to find the right answer. Failing to read all of the answer choices is like not reading all of the items on a restaurant menu. You might miss out on the perfect choice.

11. Spot the Hedges

One of the keys to success on multiple-choice tests is paying close attention to every word. This is never more true than with words like *almost, most, some,* and *sometimes.* These words are called "hedges", because they indicate that a statement is not totally true or not true in every place and time. An absolute statement will contain no hedges, but in many subjects, like literature and history, the answers are not always straightforward. There are always exceptions to the rules in these subjects. For this reason, you should favor those multiple-choice questions that contain hedging language. The presence of qualifying words indicates that the author is taking special care with his or her words, which is certainly important when composing the right answer. After all, there are many ways to be wrong, but there is only one way to be right! For this reason, it is wise when taking a multiple-choice test to avoid answers that are absolute. An absolute answer is one that says things are either all one way or all another. They often include words like *every, always, best,* and *never.* If you are taking a multiple-choice test in a subject that doesn't lend itself to absolute answers, be on your guard if you see any of these words.

12. Long Answers

In many subject areas, the answers are not simple. As already mentioned, the right answer often requires hedges. Another common feature of the answers to a complex or subjective question are qualifying clauses, which are groups of words that subtly modify the meaning of the sentence. If the question or answer choice describes a rule to which there are exceptions or the subject matter is complicated, ambiguous, or confusing, the correct answer will require many words in order to be expressed clearly and accurately. In essence, you should not be deterred by answer choices that seem excessively long. Oftentimes, the author of the text will not be able to write the correct answer without offering some qualifications and modifications. As a test taker, your job is to read the answer choices thoroughly and completely and to select the one that most accurately and precisely answers the question.

13. Restating to Understand

Sometimes, a question on a multiple-choice test is difficult not because of what it asks but because of how it is written. If this is the case, restate the question or answer choice in different words. This process serves a couple of important purposes. First, it forces you to concentrate on the core of the question. In order to rephrase the question accurately, you have to understand it well. Rephrasing the question will concentrate your mind on the key words and ideas. Second, it will present the information to your mind in a fresh way. This process may trigger your memory of some useful scrap of information picked up while studying.

14. True Statements

Sometimes an answer choice will be true in itself, but it does not answer the question. This is one of the main reasons why it is essential to read the question carefully and completely before proceeding to the answer choices. Too often, test takers skip ahead to the answer choices and look for true statements. Having found one of these, they are content to select it without reference to the question above. Obviously, this provides an easy way for test makers to play tricks. The savvy test taker will always read the entire question before turning to the answer choices. Then, having settled on a correct answer choice, he or she will refer to the original question and ensure that the selected answer is relevant. The mistake of choosing a correct-but-irrelevant answer choice is especially common on questions related to specific pieces of objective knowledge, like historical or scientific facts. A prepared test taker will have a wealth of factual knowledge at his or her disposal, but may be careless in its application.

15. No Patterns

One of the more dangerous ideas that circulate about multiple-choice tests is that the correct answers tend to fall into patterns. These erroneous ideas range from a belief that B and C are the most common right answers, to the idea that an unprepared test-taker should answer "A-B-A-C-A-D-A-B-A." It cannot be emphasized enough that pattern-seeking of this type is exactly the WRONG way to approach a multiple-choice test. To begin with, it is highly unlikely that the test maker will plot the correct answers according to some predetermined pattern. The questions are scrambled and delivered in a random order. Furthermore, even if the test maker was following a pattern in the assignation of correct answers, there is no reason why the test maker would know which pattern he or she was using. Any attempt to discern a pattern in the answer choices is a waste of time and a distraction from the real work of taking the test. A test taker would be much better served by extra preparation before the test than by reliance on a pattern in the answers.

Corrections Officer Exam

Corrections

The term "corrections" encompasses the act of incarcerating and rehabilitating offenders. It also refers to the agencies and programs that are responsible for these programs. Each state has a government agency that is responsible for the corrections function in that state. This agency operates the state's prisons and manages other corrections programs. The structure and management of these agencies varies from state-to-state.

An agency administrator, typically appointed by the governor, oversees the functions of the department. The department sets the policies that govern all of the institutions and programs under its jurisdiction. There are approximately 1,100 state confinement facilities in the United States and another 300 to 400 community corrections programs.

Criminal justice system

The criminal justice system consists of law enforcement, courts, and corrections institutions. Law enforcement is responsible for investigating crimes, gathering evidence, and making arrests. Prosecutors, who are part of law enforcement, represent the state in court, arguing for conviction and sentencing.

Courts are responsible for balancing enforcement of the law against the rights of the accused. Trial courts manage the trial of criminal matters, with a jury if requested by the accused. If the accused is found guilty, he may be sentenced to probation, a fine, or incarceration in a jail or prison. There are at least two levels of appellate court above every trial court, including the United States Supreme Court. Finally, corrections agencies are responsible for punishment and rehabilitation.

Standards

No single set of correctional standards applies throughout the United States. In 1870, the National Prison Congress met and developed the first set of principles and objectives for prison operations. This group later became the American Correctional Association (ACA), a private, non-profit organization.

The ACA has expanded those early principles and objectives into a comprehensive set of standards. Membership in the ACA is voluntary, as is compliance with the association's standards. About 10% of federal prisons and 44% of state prisons are accredited by the ACA. The Bureau of Prisons has adopted regulations and administrative procedures that provide standards for federal prisons. Some states have also adopted formal standards. The federal and states standards are based in great part on the ACA's standards.

Facility accreditation

Facility accreditation refers to a review of the prison for compliance with corrections standards. The review may be conducted by a federal, state, or local government agency or it may be conducted by a private organization, such as the ACA or its affiliate, the Commission on Accreditation for Corrections (CAC). Accreditation standards address services, programs, and operations. Factors considered typically include physical plant, safety and emergency procedures, sanitation, food service, staff training, inmate discipline, and financial operations.

In the federal prison system, or in states that have adopted accreditation standards, accreditation is mandatory. In other facilities, accreditation is voluntary and the facility itself must initiate the process by contacting the accrediting organization and requesting an audit.

National Commission on Correctional Health Care (NCCHC)

The NCCHC is a nonprofit organization created by the American Medical Association in 1970, in cooperation with a number of other organizations and associations interested in correctional health care. The NCCHC has developed voluntary, national standards for health services in prisons, jails, and juvenile facilities. The standards address care and treatment, health records, administration, personnel, and medical-legal issues.

The NCCHC offers accreditation of prison health care services, also on a voluntary basis. More recently, the NCCHC has started offering accreditation of opioid treatment programs. This accreditation allows facilities to obtain required certification from the federal Substance Abuse and Mental Health Services Administration (SAMHSA). The Commission also offers certification of prison healthcare professionals.

Audits

An audit is a review of facility or agency records or procedures. An audit may be conducted by an agency employee – an *internal* audit – or by an outside person or organization – an *external* audit. Audit goals vary widely. Financial audits are mathematical double-checks. The auditor cross-checks financial records to ensure their accuracy. Records audits also involve cross-checking, but they involve information, not finances. Finally, procedures audits check that (a) the appropriate procedures have been adopted; and (b) the adopted procedures are followed. Upon completion of the audit, the auditor prepares a report and submits it to the requesting entity. Prison audits may be requested by prison administration, a prison board of trustees, a higher-level office (such as the governor), or by the state legislature.

Male inmate population

There are about 2 million males incarcerated in the United States, the highest incarceration rate in the developed world.
- Race: About 35% of the male prison population is white, 20% is Hispanic, 36% is African-American, and 4% is Asian or other.
- Age: The majority of male inmates are between the ages of 20 and 30.
- Offense: About half of male inmates are serving time for a violent offense, 20% for a property crime (such as theft), and 20% for drugs.

In addition, about 5% of the inmates in state prison are not US citizens. The number increases to 20% in federal prisons. About 12% are serving in federal prisons, with about 60% in state prisons, and the remainder (28%) in local jails.

Female inmate population

There are about 180,000 females serving time in state and federal prisons and local jails – almost 8% of the total prison population. The incarceration rate for women is increasing faster than the incarceration rate for men.

The female prison population can be summed up by a rule of two-thirds:
- Race: roughly two thirds are minority (African-American or Hispanic)
- Age: roughly two-thirds of female inmates are less than 35 years old
- Offense: roughly two-thirds are serving time for property (e.g., theft) and drug offenses.

In addition, roughly two-thirds of female inmates are parents of minor children. About 5% of female prisoners are pregnant at the time of incarceration.

Juvenile justice corrections program

There are about 100,000 offenders in juvenile facilities. All juveniles are in state prisons, because federal prisons do not accept minors. The age at which a minor can be incarcerated with adult inmates is 18 in most states, but some states process offenders who are 17 years old as adults and a handful process offenders as young as 16 years old as adults. Once a minor is committed to a juvenile facility, he or she may remain in the system until the age of 21.

Juvenile facilities are subject to the federal Juvenile Justice and Delinquency Prevention Act, which was passed in 1974 and reauthorized in 2002. The JJDPA establishes four "protections" for minor offenders: (1) reducing commitment for status crimes (e.g., runaways); (2) separating minors from adult offenders; (3) removing minors from adult jails; and (4) reducing the disproportionate number of minorities in the system.

Problems in prison population

Inmates are more likely to be educationally-disadvantaged. About 10% have a learning or speech disability and less than one-third had completed high school at the time of incarceration.

Inmates are more likely to have mental health problems. About one-half have symptoms of mental illness or mood disorder. Approximately one in eight receives mental health services, with about ten percent receiving medicine for such conditions as depression, anxiety, and schizophrenia. In addition, about two-thirds have a history of substance abuse.

Inmates are much more likely to have communicable diseases. It is estimated that as much as 20% of the inmate population is positive for hepatitis B virus (HBV). Inmates are about 4 times as likely to test positive for tuberculosis (TB). About 3% of female and 2% of male inmates are positive for the human immunodeficiency virus (HIV). Many inmates arrive at prison infected by other sexually-transmitted diseases (STDs).

Federal prison system

The federal prison system is run by the Bureau of Prisons (BOP), an agency of the Department of Justice. The BOP is responsible for incarceration of inmates who have been convicted of federal laws and of felony violations of the Code of the District of Columbia. The BOP also administers military prisons. The BOP also contracts with private corrections companies, state prisons, and jails to handle inmates in special situations or where the federal prisons lack capacity.

The BOP includes the National Institute of Corrections (NIC). The NIC provides training, technical assistance, information services, and program development assistance to federal, state, and local institutions. NIC maintains a library of resources and information regarding corrections.

Private corrections industry

Private companies may take over the operations of government prisons, or they may build private prisons and contract with government agencies to house offenders in those prisons. Fees are calculated on a per-person, per-day basis. Private prison management was popular during the 1980s. Proponents of private prisons argue that they are more efficient and not hampered by laws and regulations applicable to government employers. Opponents argue that private prisons cut corners, are more susceptible to corruption, and are not as stable because the company operating the prison might go out of business. They also assert that the fee structure discourages early release programs. The largest private corrections firms in the United States are the Corrections Corporation of America (CCA), the GEO Group, and the Cornell Companies.

The Auburn System

The Auburn System was an approach to corrections developed at the Auburn Penitentiary in New York in the early 1800s. Its predecessor, the Pennsylvania System, involved solitary confinement of inmates so that they could reflect on their crimes. The Auburn System, by contrast, provided for communal work and eating areas, with single-occupancy cells used only for sleeping. The Auburn System carried forward the Pennsylvania System's requirement of strict silence. Moreover, harsh discipline was used to maintain order in common areas. Inmates who did not follow the rules were sent into permanent solitary confinement, which often led to mental breakdowns. The concept of cells as sleeping areas and a central common area where prisoners could congregate has been carried forward into modern times.

Boot camp

A boot camp – or regimented treatment program -- is an alternative to traditional incarceration for young, first-time offenders. Boot camps use military training techniques to "shock" or rehabilitate offenders and introduce them to structure and discipline. Boot camps are most widely used for juvenile offenders and often only the consent of the parent – and not of the inmate – is required. A short-term sentence in a boot camp can substitute for a longer sentence in a traditional prison. The overall concept is behavior modification, but boot camps may also include educational and substance abuse programs. Boot camps were outlawed in Florida in 2006 after corrections officers inadvertently suffocated an offender by putting ammonia tablets in his nostrils in an attempt to revive him after he collapsed.

Direct supervision

With modern "indirect" supervision, corrections officers are separated from inmates by physical barriers, such as a secure control booth. One or more officers monitor a "pod" of inmates and operate control systems. This technique increases officer safety, but its efficacy as an inmate management technique has been questioned. With direct supervision, a corrections officer works in a pod with the inmates to manage their behavior. The officer moves throughout the unit and usually uses a desk in the common area, rather than a secure control booth. Therefore, the officer has direct contact with each inmate. The officer is responsible for recognizing and defusing problems before they get out of hand.

Unit management approach

Unit management is a team approach to corrections, started by the Bureau of Prisons. It is now used it virtually every federal prison. The prison is divided into groups of 200 to 300 inmates. Management and decision-making performed on a unit basis, with each unit operating as a mini-prison within the larger facility. Multidisciplinary teams consisting of unit managers, caseworkers, officers, and other professionals are assigned to each unit and office in the unit. Each inmate remains in the unit for most of his sentence. The increased and long-term contact between inmates and staff fosters interpersonal relationships. Moreover, staff is able to make more knowledgeable decisions about treatment and specialized programs for each inmate.

Communicating policies to inmates

Upon arrival, each inmate should be provided with a copy of the unit's rules and regulations and the institution's policies should be reviewed with the inmate. In addition, each housing unit should have a method of communicating the following information:

- Inmate rights and responsibilities;
- Inmate grievance policy;
- Housekeeping policy and procedures;
- Hygiene and personal appearance policy;
- Personal property matrix;
- Inmate mail policy;
- Disciplinary rules and sanctions for violations;
- Fire evacuation plan;
- Visitation rules and schedule;
- Program and activity schedule;
- Schedule for religious services;
- Escorted leave schedule;
- Other relevant information.

This information may be posted on a bulletin board in the common area.

Emergency plans

An emergency plan should address the following:

- Definition: The plan should specify what constitutes an "emergency" and who has authority to declare an emergency. The list will usually include any situation where there is threat to human life, large-scale destruction of property, or a risk of loss of control of the institution. The list may also include major labor problems, such as a strike, and natural disasters.
- Response: The plan should set forth steps for responding to the emergency, including establishing a command post, chain of command, and assistance from outside agencies.
- Notifications: The plan should specify who is to be notified outside of the prison when there is an emergency. This includes notices to the media, where appropriate.
- Training: The plan should set forth the annual training requirements, including the types of training and how often training will occur.

Civil disturbances

A civil disturbance is unrest outside of the institution, involving civilians, such as a protest or riot. The disturbance may be directed at the institution, such as death penalty protests, or it may be unrelated, such as the riots in Los Angeles after the Rodney King verdict.

Civil disturbances pose three types of risk to the institution. First, the disturbance might block access to the institution, creating problems with staffing and supplies. Second, civilians might target the institution for violence, or the disturbance may disrupt vital resources, such as electricity. Third, the disturbance may spread to the inmates, or may cause stress or concern among the inmates. The institution should have a civil disturbance plan that addresses each of these risks. The plan should address communications with outside law enforcement and the authority of corrections officers to arrest civilians who enter the institution.

Work or food strikes

Work or food strikes signal serious discontent among inmates. In a large-scale strike, the fact that inmates are acting in concert increases the risk that the strike will progress to a mass disturbance. Accordingly, the institution should respond quickly to identify the reason for the protest and address inmate concerns to the extent possible. First, officers should be alert to signs of an impending strike. Hunger strikes are often announced in advance. Second, officers should determine the cause of the strike and should identify the strike's leaders. Third, inmates should be encouraged to use the institution's grievance procedure to address their complaints. Fourth, health care personnel should be alerted to the risk of a hunger strike as early as possible so that they can monitor the mental and physical status of the inmates.

Mass staff sick call or staff strikes

Administration will have to address staff complaints while maintaining institution security. First, administration should determine the source of staff discontent as soon as possible and take appropriate action to address the complaints. Staff should be encouraged to use formal grievance procedures. Second, administration should address institution security. Staffing should be analyzed to determine which posts can be temporarily shut down and which programs can be suspended without adverse effect on inmate morale and security. Third, administration should address other sources of personnel. Staff members who continue to report to work may be called on to work extra hours. Administration may also be able to obtain assistance from other institutions or law enforcement. Fifth, administration should communicate with inmates about the status of the strike and should be alert to inmates who will try to take advantage of the situation.

Natural or civil disasters

A natural disaster (tornado, hurricane, earthquake, etc.) or civil disaster (bombing or declaration of war) may threaten the physical plant of the institution and cause stress to inmates. It can also disrupt staffing and supplies. The institution should have in place a plan that addresses:

- Information: Administration, or a designee, should remain in contact with outside authorities throughout the situation to make sure that the institution has current information.
- Internal Communication: Administration should regularly communicate status to staff and inmates and provide updates as appropriate.
- Records Protection: The plan should address preservation of records that could affect the rights of any person.
- Evacuation: The plan should set forth procedures for evacuation.
- Staffing and supplies: The plan should address procedures for dealing with staffing shortages, along the lines of the institution's plan for dealing with a staff strike, supply shortages, and disruption of utilities.

Housekeeping plans

The housekeeping plan should address common areas, cells, and inmate hygiene:
- Common areas: Inmates should be assigned cleaning duties in the common areas.
- Cells: Cells should be cleaned daily, including making the bed, and picking litter and debris up off the floor. Inmates should be in compliance with the institution's policy regarding personal property.
- Inmate hygiene: All inmates should have access to toilet facilities and hot and cold running water 24 hours a day. The plan should address showering. The institution should provide hair care services.
- Inmate laundry: The plan should address access to laundry facilities within the institution or nearby.
- Inspections: The plan should provide for inspection of common areas and cells at least once each week.
- Discipline: The plan, or another policy, should set forth the discipline for violations of housekeeping and hygiene standards.

Bomb plans

A bomb plan should address the following:
- Threat reporting: Most bomb threats are received by telephone, but threats may also be sent in writing through the mail or e-mail. Staff should document the nature of the threat, the means by which it was communicated, the time and date of receipt, and any other useful information.
- Communication: Staff should alert law enforcement and should also inform all staff members if a bomb is located or if a bomb threat is received.
- Detection: The plan should address the response if an officer locates a bomb or suspected bomb. Officers should never attempt to move a bomb. The plan should address reducing sources of electrical energy or radio signals in the prison that might activate the bomb.
- Evacuation: The plan should address evacuation of inmates and staff.
- Training: The plan should specify any required training regarding bombs and bomb threats.

Mass disturbance plans

A *mass disturbance* or *riot* is one of the most serious crises for a corrections institution due the risk of personal injury, property destruction, and loss of control. The plan should address:
- Communication: The incident should immediately be communicated within the unit, institution, and department. The plan should also address communication to outside authorities and, where appropriate, the media.
- Command: The chain of command should be clearly set forth. Commanders should provide for isolation of the disturbance as soon as possible.
- Staffing: Circumstances under which additional staff should be called in to assist should be specified.
- Assault team: An assault team should be assembled to retake control. The plan should address tactical methods.
- Regular operations: The plan should identify who will be responsible for maintaining normal operations in the rest of the facility so that other inmates do not suffer due to the actions of those participating in the disturbance.

Procedures for restoring normalcy after a mass disturbance should address inmate needs, physical plant, staff needs, investigation and discipline, and a report.

- Inmates: There should be a full count of inmates in the institution. Medical personnel should be available to address medical and psychological issues.
- Physical plant: Areas that were damaged, where gas was used, or that are otherwise not habitable should be evacuated. Arrangements should be made for facility repairs and replacement of any destroyed property.
- Staff needs: There should be a full count of staff. Medical personnel should be available to address medical and psychological issues.
- Investigation and discipline: There should be a full investigation and evidence should be collected. Discipline proceedings should be conducted for all those involved.
- Report: A full report should be prepared. The report should address any recommended changes to procedures.

Escape plans

An escape plan should address:

- Confirmation and containment: Officers should confirm that one or more inmates are missing. A full inmate count should be conducted and the facility should be thoroughly searched. A suspected escape should be reported throughout the institution immediately, especially to perimeter guards.
- Escapee identification packet: Once the escape is confirmed, an identification packet should be assembled on each missing inmate.
- Notification: A suspected escape should immediately be reported to administration. The plan should specify which outside agencies should be notified of the escape, including state and local law enforcement and, where appropriate, the media. Victim notification procedures should be followed. "Wanted" flyers should be posted and distributed.
- Escapee recovery: The plan should specify procedures for assembling recovery teams, use of fugitive apprehension agents, and jurisdictional issues.
- Escape warrant: The district attorney should be contacted about filing escape charges.

Hostage plans

A hostage plan should address the following:

- Communication: Officers should report hostage situations immediately to a supervisor. The officer who first learns of the situation should not attempt to negotiate with the hostage taker. The plan should specify procedures for notifying the hostage's family members.
- Negotiation team: The plan should identify a negotiation team. Members of the team should receive specialized training.
- Loss of authority: The plan should specify that any employee taken hostage immediately loses any administrative authority to issue directives to others.
- Non-negotiable matters: The plan should set forth any items that are not negotiable, such as release.
- Hostage training: All staff members should be trained on appropriate hostage behavior.
- Institution security: The plan should specify any special security measures that will be observed, such as securing the area and putting the remainder of the institution under lock-down or other special status.

ACA standards for fire prevention

The ACA standards for fire protection address the following:
- Inspections: The standards require regular equipment inspections by internal personnel and inspection by external authorities at least once each year.
- Training: Staff should be trained in the use of fire extinguishers and basic fire suppression techniques. The institution should pursue joint training exercises with local firefighting agencies. Joint exercises at the institution allow outside firefighters to become familiar with the facility's layout.
- Equipment: The standard calls for safety equipment pursuant to the Life Safety Code of the National Fire Protection Association, including extinguishers, hoses, nozzles, water supplies, and sprinklers. The institution should have access to a fire truck.
- Alarms: The institution should have adequate emergency alarms, smoke detectors, and equipment to notify hearing- and vision-impaired inmates.
- Evacuation plan: Each facility should have a written evacuation plan. A certified inspector should review the plan.

Fire plans

A fire plan should address the following:
- Notification: The plan should list persons to be contacted -- internal and external – in the event of a fire
- Personnel: Each facility should have at least one designated staff member who is responsible for compliance with the fire plan. In addition, the plan should set forth eligibility criteria for inmates to serve as fire crew.
- Equipment: Each institution should have adequate safety equipment, including extinguishers and hoses.
- Inspections: Safety equipment should be inspected regularly.
- Evacuation: Each facility should have a diagram of fire evacuation routes.
- Security: The plan should set forth security procedures during an evacuation.
- Training: All employees should receive training on the fire plan and the evacuation routes.
- Drills: Fire drills should be conducted at least one time each month. Inmates should participate to the extent feasible.

Preventing fires is easier than suppressing them. Prevention strategies include:
- Smoking: Non-combustible receptacles should be provided in outside smoking areas, as well as inside, if smoking is permitted indoors.
- Flammable liquids: Inmates should use flammable liquids only under supervision and in the minimum quantities possible. Storage cabinets should be fireproof. Rags used with flammable liquids should be disposed of in non-combustible containers.
- Electrical hazards: Inmates and employees should be alert to altered or overloaded electrical outlets. Unauthorized appliances and extension cords also pose a hazard.
- Trash: Proper storage and disposal of trash is necessary to reduce the amount of combustible material.
- Mattresses: Especially where inmates are allowed to smoke indoors, mattresses should be of a material that meets the flammability standards set forth in the Life Safety Code.

Utility failure plans

A utility failure plan should include the following:

- Definition: The plan should distinguish between minimal or isolated utility failures and severe utility failures – those that impact safety, health, or welfare of staff or inmates.
- Notification: The plan should provide for notification of administration if there is a severe utility failure, including the identification of the administrator responsible for determining whether additional staff or equipment is necessary. The plan should provide for notifying the utility provider.
- Vital operations: The plan should identify those utility-dependent functions at each facility – such as electrical fences -- that cannot be interrupted. Provisions should be made to maintain continuity of these functions during a utility failure. Electricity generating equipment should be available for vital functions.
- Utility diagrams: Diagrams of utility systems should be accessible to facility location of the problem and repairs.

Prison chaplains

Prison chaplains are the spiritual counselors of the correctional system. Chaplains are typically staff officers, paid by the county or state that runs the prison. In some states, the chaplain function is outsourced. There may be one, two, or more chaplains assigned to a prison, and these employees may work either full- or part-time.

The qualifications for prison chaplains vary, but most institutions require at least a four-year college degree and religious training, either formal or informal. Some institutions also require chaplains to have experience with counseling.

Prison chaplains must usually have "denominational endorsement," which is support from a specific, organized religion. However, all chaplains are expected to be "interdenominational." This means they must provide religious support for all of the religions practiced by inmates.

The general duties of prison chaplains fall into the following categories: religious services, religious education, counseling, coordination of internal staff, coordination of external resources, and public relations.

Prison chaplains conduct interdenominational religious services for all inmates. They are also responsible for religious education. In this respect, chaplains maintain libraries of religious books and other resources for inmates of all religions.

Prison chaplains counsel inmates, their families, and even staff members. If there is a death in an inmate's family, the prison chaplain is responsible for breaking the news to the inmate and providing grief counseling. Prison chaplains also counsel inmates who are suicidal. They receive letters from inmate families and they counsel family members who come to visit inmates.

Prison chaplains coordinate resources, both internal and external. Internally, a prison chaplain may have a staff. The chaplain will also work closely with the corrections officers in the institution, relying on them for information about inmates who need special assistance. Externally, the prison chaplain will respond to inquiries from outside ministers and arrange for their visits to the prison.

Prison chaplains must balance their duties as spiritual advisors with their correctional responsibilities. As staff officers, prison chaplains may be called on to advise management about security matters. This may include arranging security passes for inmates who wish to attend services or security so an inmate can attend the funeral of a close relative.

As spiritual advisors, prison chaplains must be neutral about the religious choices of the inmates, while providing guidance and support. This means chaplains must support, and not disparage, each inmate's religion. Prison chaplains provide or arrange for religious ceremonies, such as baptism, communion, and last rites.

To establish relationships with inmates, chaplains circulate throughout the prison on a regular basis, including the yard, visiting areas, and the infirmary. They also maintain offices where inmates can counsel in private.

Like the chaplain, the corrections officer must maintain a balance between the religious rights of inmates and the officer's correctional responsibilities. Corrections staff must never disparage any matter relating to inmate religious practices, including an inmate's religion, religious practices, religious services at the prison, and the prison chaplain. Moreover, corrections officers should recognize that the chaplain is an important source of support for inmates. Officers should encourage inmates who are going through unusually tough times or difficulties to visit the prison chaplain. In some cases, it may be appropriate to ask the chaplain to check on a particular inmate.

On the other hand, officers are responsible for providing security, even during religious services. Most institutions require an officer to be present during services. An officer assigned to chapel duty should maintain neutrality and not interfere with the services unless there is a security problem.

Finally, officers should respect the confidences between chaplains and the inmates. Chaplains' conversations with inmates are confidential. Chaplains do not have a duty to disclose their conversations with inmates unless necessary to prevent serious injury to the inmates or others. Accordingly, officer should not ask or expect chaplains to disclose their conversations with inmates.

Corrections office job positions

A corrections officer is responsible for maintaining security and order in an assigned area. This may include cellblocks, the yard, classrooms, the chapel, and work areas. New officers may be assigned to posts with limited inmate contact. They work under close supervision and have little or no authority to make independent judgments.

As officers gain experience and confidence, they progress to more inmate contact and direct inmate custody. More senior officers rotate through supervision of work detail, living quarters, recreational activities, and other inmate activities. Assignments requiring advanced skills include intake, work release, dealing with inmates with serious behavior problems, structured treatment, and rehabilitation programs. Some senior officers may also have responsibility for training new officers.

Corrections officer rights and duties

Officers of the law have the same rights and privileges afforded to every citizen by the Constitution. Officers are free to join labor unions, and may enjoy federal protections in this capacity. There are also a number of other laws specifically designed to protect the rights of state and federal employees. These include the Family Medical Leave Act, which gives employees the right to take medical leave, and the Fair Labor Standards Act, which describes when employees are owed overtime pay.

The standard duties of all officers are:
- Work Ethic: Officers must demonstrate strong work ethics. An officer should always be alert and attentive to duty: he should avoid distractions and notify a supervisor if he becomes sleepy or otherwise impaired while on duty.
- Relationships with Inmates: Officers must keep relationships with inmates on a professional level. Personal relationships undermine authority and security. For example, officers should not use nicknames when addressing inmates, give inmates gifts, accept anything from an inmate, or grant special privileges. If an officer recognizes an inmate or otherwise realizes that the officer knew the inmate before the inmate was incarcerated, the officer should report this to a supervisor.
- Monitoring of Inmates: Officers must be alert to changes in the prison community. An officer should note unusual activities or changes in daily routine, conduct, or appearance of one or more inmates. The officer should document these changes and report them to a supervisor.

Corrections officer responsibilities

The standard responsibilities of all officers are:
- Respect for Authority: Officers must maintain respect for authority. The conduct of officers sets an example for inmates. Officers should address one another, and superiors, professionally and should respect the chain of command.
- Reliability: Officers must be reliable. They must report to work on time and respond immediately when called in for overtime or during an emergency. If an officer is impaired in any manner, he should immediately tell a supervisor. Once at work, officers must remain at their posts until the next shift reports for duty.
- Personal Security: In addition to their responsibility for prison security, officers must maintain personal security. By wearing regulation uniforms, employees identify themselves as officers. Moreover, officers are responsible for their personal items. An officer should secure his personal vehicle in the parking lot and should not bring any personal items to work unless absolutely necessary. When the officer arrives at his post, he should inspect the equipment and report any problems to a supervisor.

Corrections officers' rights

The rights of corrections officers depend on where they work. All officers are protected by the United States Constitution and federal laws, such as the Fair Labor Standards Act (minimum wage and overtime pay), that apply to all employees. Depending on the number of employees at the institution, officers may also be protected by Title VII, the Age Discrimination in Employment Act, and the Americans with Disabilities Act (anti-discrimination laws), and the Family Medical Leave Act.

In federal facilities and non-"right to work" states (such as Texas), officers may also be members of a union and have rights under a collective bargaining agreement (union contract). Moreover, even right-to-work states have laws protecting whistleblowers and workers' compensation claimants, among other things. An officer should become familiar with the labor laws in his or her state.

Code of Ethics

The Code of Ethics is a set of guiding principles, promulgated by the ACA, for corrections officers. It does not have the force of law unless it has been adopted into law by a particular state or other jurisdiction. However, it provides a frame of reference for corrections officers in carrying out their professional duties. Moreover, it extends to institutions and corrections officers who are members of the ACA.

In addition, many states and penal institutions have their own codes of ethics. States often require public employees to adhere to rules regarding conflicts of interest – relating to financial relationships -- and nepotism – relating to employment of relatives. These rules have the force of law and often carry criminal, as well as civil, penalties. An officer should be familiar with the applicable ethical rules in his state.

Part one: The Code declares that all corrections officers should make an effort to respect the civil and legal rights of other people at all times. Members of the ACA should never seek personal gain, but should make the benefit of other people the motivation for their professional activities. They should maintain solid working relationships with their colleagues in order to improve professional practice. They should avoid criticizing their colleagues publicly unless the criticism is warranted, constructive, and verifiable. They should respect the various disciplines at work in the criminal justice system, and should promote understanding between them. They should share information with the public as much as possible, so long as it does not infringe on the privacy of anyone

Part two: Members of the ACA are encouraged by the Code of Ethics to protect the rights of the members of the general public to be shielded from criminal activity. They should never use their professional position to obtain personal privileges, and should not allow personal interest to interfere with the performance of their duties. They should never enter into any situation that presents a possible conflict of interest, and should not accept any gifts or services that are improper or imply an obligation inconsistent with the effective and objective performance of duty. They should immediately report any corrupt or unethical behavior to the appropriate authorities.

Part three: Members of the American Corrections Association should always draw distinction between their personal views and the positions they take on behalf of an institution or the ACA. Members should never discriminate against any person because of that person's race, gender, creed, nationality, age, disability, or religious affiliation. They should preserve the integrity of private information and refrain from seeking any more information than is absolutely necessary to perform their duties. Members should make any necessary appointments, promotions, or dismissals according to the prevailing civil service rules, and on the basis of merit rather than personal interest. Finally, members of the ACA should always promote a workplace that is safe and healthy for all employees.

Ethical principals

The guiding principle for corrections officers is professionalism. Officers must balance their professional duties with their obligations toward inmates and their responsibilities to the public. In doing so, corrections officers are guided by the following ethical principles:
- promote respect for the profession
- respect other members of the criminal justice system
- report corrupt or unethical behavior
- refrain from using the officer's position for personal gain
- refrain from activities that are improper or have the appearance of impropriety
- refrain from accepting gifts or favors that may compromise the officer's professional duties
- do not engage in discrimination
- respect individual rights
- respect the public's right to information
- protect the public from criminal activity

Unethical behaviors

Unethical behaviors could include any of the following:
- Engaging in personal transactions with inmates or inmate relatives: selling, trading, bartering, giving, or receiving goods or services of any kind. This activity can compromise an officer's objectivity.
- Personal involvement with an inmate: familiarity with inmates can compromise an officer's objectivity. Officers should remain professional at all time and should not discuss their personal issues with inmates.
- Being under the influence of drugs or alcohol: intoxicants of any kind can delay reaction and impair an officer's effectiveness and judgment.
- Bringing contraband into the institution: Officers should not introduce contraband into the prison environment, including personal firearms, sharps, and personal electronic devices. This conduct creates unnecessary risk and contributes to the difficulty of controlling contraband within the institution.
- Fiscal improprieties, including the theft and misuse of inmate or institutional funds
- Abuse of inmates, whether physical, emotional, or sexual
- Inappropriate relationships with inmates, including bribery, conflict of interest, solicitation of gifts or favors
- On-duty misconduct, including insubordination, inattention to duty, breach of security, loss of temper, and gambling
- Off-duty misconduct, including any behavior that would adversely affect the officer's ability to perform his or her professional duties
- Investigative violations, including any attempts to cover up misconduct

Recognizing unethical behavior

Unethical behavior is often hard to detect, but an officer should be alert to indicators:
- Fraternization: on officer who is unduly familiar with inmates or employees of other law enforcement agencies
- Complaints: a pattern of complaints about an officer, an area of the institution, or supplies
- Lack of interest: an officer who seems uninterested in his work and is not responsive to legitimate needs of inmates
- Personal problems: an officer who has legal (civil, criminal), financial, physical, or mental problems

The proper reaction to unethical conduct should depend on the frequency and severity. Possible responses include:

- Expressing verbal disapproval
- Discussing continued problems with a supervisor
- Reporting violations to a supervisor
- Preventing criminal violations.

Whenever a credible complaint is made about an officer, the supervisor should investigate it fully. If it is determined that the complaint constitutes a criminal offense, the investigation should be turned over to another law enforcement agency. Once the evidence has been accumulated, it should only be given out as is necessary, and all witnesses should be required to sign an affidavit. If it will provide evidence, the subject in question may be put under surveillance. This surveillance may include peer monitoring, audiotape, or videotape. Near the end of the investigation, the subject should be interviewed. At all times, the rights of inmates and officers should be respected and protected.

"Code of silence"

The "code of silence" refers to an unwritten rule among officers to not report violations and to retaliate against those who do. It is widely recognized as one of the most serious problems facing the profession. The following methods are suggestions for breaking the "code of silence":

- Clarify that each employee's responsibilities include enforcements of rules, regulations, and ethical principals
- Adopt a clear mission statement and connect each employee's job to it
- Require accountability at all levels, enforced through regular audits
- Adopt a code of conduct and discipline sanctions for those who violate it
- Provide a means to report violations, anonymously if necessary

In addition, the highest levels of management must set an example through conduct that is without reproach.

Supervisor duties

Supervisors must be able to manage and communicate with their staff. Staff management includes planning staffing levels, scheduling post assignments, monitoring compliance with policies and procedures, managing supplies of equipment, providing feedback, formal and informal, administering staff discipline, and conducting written performance evaluations. Supervisors are also responsible for scheduling training for staff and participating in training themselves. In some cases, a supervisor may lead a training session.

Staff communication includes: making sure that the staff knows policies and procedures, communicating updates or changes to those policies and procedures, facilitating communication between shifts, and communicating to all staff about problems with inmates. Supervisors must also listen to complaints about staff and conduct or arrange for investigations.

As with their staffs, supervisors manage and communicate with inmates. They are responsible for ensuring enforcement of institution policies and rules with respect to inmates. They must maintain a presence in the facility and establish a rapport with inmates, so that inmates will approach them with questions or concerns. They may also authorize and schedule inmate programs.

Supervisors monitor inmate counts, manage inmate movement, and assist with restraint situations. They conduct security, safety, and health inspections. Supervisors also participate in determining classifications and may be required to testify at disciplinary and release proceedings. They are responsible for written reports and documentation of incidents.

Supervisors manage crises. The mediate disputes between inmates and staff or between inmates, and they initiate emergency procedures.

Chain of command

The term "chain of command," which originated in the military, refers to the hierarchical structure of authority and responsibility. Generally, one person in the chain of command take orders only from the person immediately above him and gives orders only to those below him. Corrections officers in prisons follow the chain of command system.

In a chain of command system, the manager in charge of the line personnel is called a "front line supervisor." If a line employee has a complaint, he is required to address the complaint first to a front line supervisor. If the front line supervisor is unresponsive, the employee is permitted to go to the next person in the chain of command.

Firearms

A corrections officer may use a rifle, a shotgun, or a handgun. A rifle is a long-barreled, single-shot firearm. A shotgun is a long-barreled, multiple-shot firearm. Under most circumstances, two hands are required for operation of a long-barreled firearm. A handgun is a pistol or similar firearm that can be held and operated with one hand.

Each of these firearms has advantages and disadvantages. Handguns are small and so easier to carry. However, they are not very accurate. Rifles are more accurate, but they fire only one bullet. Shotguns spray pellets, and so cover a large area. For this reason, a shotgun may hit more than the intended target.

In the corrections context, the goal is to slow down or scare the target, not to cause serious injury. For this reason, the best strategy is often to shoot near the target or at the ground by the target.

Pat-down search procedures

Procedures for pat-down searches vary from institution to institution. Thus, the most important thing is to make sure you know the procedures that apply to your job.

There are some things that most pat-downs searches have in common. The inmate should be instructed to remove any loose items from his pockets or clothing for inspection. The inmate should also remove any outer layers of clothing, such as hats, sweaters, and coats.

After these steps, the officer uses his open hand to pat down the outer layer of the inmate's clothing and the inmate's person to determine whether the inmate has any contraband. The officer should be alert the possibility that the inmate is concealing needles or other sharp objects in his clothing. In the corrections setting, the officer may also wear latex gloves during the search.

Inmate intake procedures

Intake procedures address identification, orientation, assessment of needs and risks, and case management. The officer should confirm the identity of the inmate, and take photographs and fingerprints. The officer should provide the inmate with the institution's rules and procedures, as well as the prison address for correspondence. The inmate should be searched for contraband and his possessions inventoried. The inmate should be provided clothing and supplies and assigned housing.

The officer should determine the security level of the inmate, whether the inmate is a member of a security threat group (gang), and whether the inmate needs protection from any other inmates. Medical, mental health, education, and substance abuse testing should be conducted. The inmate should be interviewed and his file reviewed to determine case management strategy.

Pre-service and in-service training

Training is a structured activity designed to achieve specific learning objective(s). It may be classroom-based on involve pen and paper tests, it may involve hands-on training, at the job site, or it may include a physical component, such as firearms or self-defense training.

Before a corrections officer begins duty, he will go through "pre-service" training. Pre-service training covers the philosophy, methods, and techniques of corrections. It usually lasts several weeks and covers the basic functions of the corrections officer's job.

In-service training, on the other hand, is conducted after the officer has begun duty. Most employers require a certain amount of in-service training each year. In-service training may provide a review of basic skills and facility policies, introduce new procedures, or it may focus on a special area, such as working with inmates with special needs.

Occupational stress

Corrections officers work under stressful conditions. This stress comes not only from the challenges of working with inmates but also from the institution itself and from the general population, which tends to negatively stereotype corrections officers. Occupational stress can cause mental and physical damages and can lead to burnout – a feeling of hopelessness, frustration, and detachment.

Management must encourage personal and professional development. A stress awareness program can help officers manage their stress by acknowledging their feelings and learning visualization and breathing exercises. Another important strategy is career development. Corrections officers frequently cite a lack of professional opportunities as a source of job stress. Career development involves identifying the officer's desired career path in corrections and mapping out a plan for the officer to achieve his objectives. The plan will identify the sequence of steps the officer must take as well as any educational or licensure requirements.

Sexual harassment

Sexual harassment occurs when sexual behavior is proposed as a condition of employment, or if one worker's sexual conduct intrudes into the lives of other workers. Anytime that the sexual conduct of one person has an adverse effect on the ability of another person to do his or her job, sexual harassment has occurred. Anytime sexual advances contribute to a hostile work environment, this can be defined as sexual harassment.

There are two types of sexual harassment. With *quid pro quo harassment*, the employee is expect to accept the harassment in return for a job benefit, such as a promotion, a raise, or merely retaining his or her job. Quid pro quo harassment is, by definition, committed by a supervisor or other member of management who has the ability to confer or withhold the job benefit.

Hostile environment harassment occurs when the workplace is so contaminated with sexual images, comments, and innuendoes as to interfere with the employee's ability to do her work. Supervisors, co-workers, and even visitors and inmates can create a hostile environment. However, a single incident of harassment does not create a hostile environment unless the harassment is severe. Moreover, the employee has an obligation to report hostile environment harassment to provide management an opportunity to address the situation.

Security classifications

Institutions are categorized based on the security level of inmate they can serve. The basic levels of facility security are the same as for inmate classifications: minimum, medium, and maximum. In addition, some prison systems recognize a level called "close security," which is between maximum and medium security, and almost all systems have a pre-release level. There are also a growing number of facilities, or units within facilities, that are designated as "supermax." There are no universal definitions of these terms. What constitutes "maximum security" in one jurisdiction may be "medium security" in another jurisdiction.

The federal Bureau of Prisons uses the terms "low security" interchangeably with "minimum security," and refers to these facilities as "camps." In addition, the BOP operates "administrative facilities," which are the rough equivalent of supermax prisons.

Minimum-security facilities – sometimes called Level II – are the next-to-lowest security level. They are used for inmates who are not considered to pose a threat of violence or escape. They are typically white-collar criminals or those with only a short time remaining on their sentences. Housing is dormitory style with communal sanitary facilities. Prisoners may move freely throughout the facility and, in some cases, may leave the campus during the day on release programs. Prisoners in these facilities are often used as labor in the higher security facilities.

Minimum security facilities may be surrounded by a fence, instead of a wall. Some have a clearly-marked perimeter instead of a fence. Guards usually are not armed.

Medium-security facilities – sometimes called Level III – usually house nonviolent offenders. Housing is typically dormitory-style, but some facilities may have cells. Sanitary facilities are usually communal. Inmates are generally locked in their sleeping quarters for 10 to 12 hours per day, but are allowed to leave their cells to eat and for recreation, education, and counseling purposes. Inmates are allowed some freedom of movement within the facility, often through a pass system. Medium-security facilities often have a small number of single-cell units that are used for discipline, i.e., solitary confinement. The facility itself is typically surrounded by one or two walls, with armed guards posted at watch towers. The walls usually have razor wire on top to prevent escape. Internal security may be managed through electronic surveillance.

Maximum-security facilities: Maximum-security facilities – sometimes called Level V – have a very high level of security, both in terms of individual inmate housing and perimeter controls. These facilities are used for inmates who present the highest risk to society, staff, and other inmates. Cells are typically single or double occupancy, with sanitary facilities inside the cell to reduce the need to move inmates. Inmates are usually locked in their cells for 23 hours per day. Inmates must be escorted by officers when moving throughout the facility.

As for perimeter control, maximum-security facilities are usually continuously patrolled by armed guards. They typically have double or even triple walls, including razor wire and/or electrical fencing with a fatal level of voltage.

Supermax facilities: Supermax is the highest security level and is used for inmates who have had discipline problems in other facilities, inmates who are known threats, and high-profile inmates. Confinement in a supermax facility is similar to solitary confinement, with single-occupancy cells and in-cell sanitary facilities. Inmates are allowed out of their cells for one hour each day to exercise in a small, cement pen. All staff-to-inmate interaction, including religious services, is done through the cell bars. Full restraint is used for any movement of the inmate, internal or external.

The supermax facility may contain unusual security measures. Cells at the BOP's supermax facility in Florence, Colorado are almost soundproof and drainpipes are routed to a central damping area, to prevent communication between inmates. No physical contact is permitted with visitors – inmates speak with visitors over the telephone. Access to the facility is through a tunnel.

Security measures

Higher security prisons have protected perimeters and limited points of entry. Perimeters are protected by physical barriers, namely two to three fences or walls spaced 20 to 30 feet apart. Razor wire may be used on top of or between the walls. Armed guards monitor the perimeter from towers set at regular intervals. The facility may also use mobile patrols – guards who patrol the outside of the perimeter by motorized vehicle.

In addition, higher security prisons have a limited number of entrances for vehicles and personnel, usually no more than one or two, as well as gates between the administrative areas and the inmate areas of the institution. Finally, all vehicles that enter or leave the premises are subjected to inspection, including inspection of the undercarriage of the vehicle.

"Sally ports"

A sally port is a double-gated entrance to a facility. The gates are operated by a guard in a secure area, using remote controls. Only one gate is opened at a time, allowing the person or vehicle to enter as far as the second gate. The first gate is then closed. In this way, the visitor is held between the gates while the person and/or vehicle is searched and authorization is confirmed. After the inspection is complete, the second gate is opened and the visitor is allowed to enter the facility. Because the first gate was closed after the visitor, there is no opening through which inmates can escape. If any problems arise while the visitor is held in between the two gates, the guard can lock down both gates and hold the visitor securely.

Control centers and safety vestibules

Both a control center and a safety vestibule are designed to provide physical barriers inside of a corrections facility. A control center is a secure, enclosed area that houses critical controls, such as fire alarms, and gate and door controls. The control center may also house keys to restricted areas.

A safety vestibule, on the other hand, is the equivalent of an internal sally port. It is an enclosed area, access to which is controlled by a series of two doors or gates, usually operated by remote control. The doors or gates are used to slow down traffic between the two areas connected by the vestibule and to ensure that only authorized persons move between those two areas.

Writ of detainer

A writ is an order issued by a court or an administrative body. A writ of detainer is similar to an arrest warrant in that it directs an institution to hold a person. A law enforcement agency may issue a writ of detainer to a corrections institution asking the institution to hold an inmate until the inmate can be transferred to the custody of the agency. An agency may also issue a writ of detainer to direct the institution to notify the agency if the person is about to be released. For this reason, an institution may have a practice or procedure of checking for writs of detainer before releasing an inmate from the institution. A writ of detainer is different from an arrest warrant because the person against whom it is directed is already in custody.

Felonies and misdemeanors

Both felonies and misdemeanors are criminal offenses, but felonies are more serious than misdemeanors. In most states, felonies are punishable by imprisonment for more than one year. Violent crimes are crimes against the person, such as murder and assault with bodily injury; they are usually felonies. Serious drug crimes and property crimes (theft and burglary) may also be felonies. Everything that is not a felony is a misdemeanor.

In most states, a person who has been convicted of a felony is "disenfranchised," meaning that the person loses the right to vote. In all but two states, convicted felons who are currently in prison are not allowed to vote. Some states reinstate voting rights after the convicted felon has completed his or her sentence. Other states provide that convicted felons lose the right to vote permanently.

Probation and parole

Both probation and parole involve supervised release of an offender. Probation is imposed after the offender is convicted, but before he is incarcerated. The offender is sentenced, but the sentence is suspended while the offender is put on probation. Parole is imposed after the offender has been incarcerated, but before the offender has completed his sentence.

In either case, the offender must meet regularly with an official to review his status. If the offender violates certain conditions, the offender is sent to prison, in the case of probation, or is returned to prison, in the case of parole. Probation and parole, along with other programs for supervision of inmates who are not currently incarcerated, are referred to as "community corrections."

Nolle prosequi and *nolo contendere*

Nolle prosequi – commonly referred to as "nol-pros" – is a decision by the prosecutor not to pursue a criminal charge. The benefit of a nol-pros is it does not count as a prosecution for double jeopardy purposes. Accordingly, a prosecutor may drop charges to avoid the bar of double jeopardy.

Nolo contendere – commonly referred to as "nolo" or "no contest" – is a decision by the accused not to fight the charges. The accused does not admit guilt by pleading guilty. He is, however, subject to the full range of sentencing. Moreover, in some states the accused is barred from appealing the sentence. The benefit of a nolo plea is that it is not an admission of guilt for civil purposes, such as where the victim sues the accused for money damages.

Adjudication

The term adjudication refers to a court's determination on the charges in a criminal case. There are many types of adjudications. A *conviction* is a determination that the accused is guilty of the crime. An *acquittal* is a determination that the accused is not guilty. A *dismissal* occurs either as a result of a *nolle prosequi* or because the court determines that there is insufficient evidence to even hold the accused over for trial. Most states use different terms for the adjudication of minors. A juvenile who is found to have committed a crime may be adjudicated a "delinquent." or "in need of supervision."

Deferred adjudication is a suspension of charges. As with probation, the accused must comply with certain conditions. If the accused completes the period of deferred adjudication without incident, the charges are dropped.

Expunction and deferred adjudication

Deferred adjudication is a suspension of charges before conviction. The accused must comply with a set of conditions, such as not incurring any more criminal charges for a period of time. If the accused violates the conditions, the charges are prosecuted. The benefit of deferred adjudication is that successful completion of the conditions results in no record of a conviction. However, the arrest may remain on the record of the accused.

Expunction – also called expungement – is the removal of criminal charges after an adjudication other than guilt. For example, an expunction may be available after a *nolle prosequi* dismissal of the charges. In some cases, such as with minors, an expunction may be available after the sentence has been served, if the accused maintains a clean criminal record for an extended period of time. A court order is usually required for an expunction.

Sentencing guidelines

The federal government and most states have adopted guidelines for judges to use in setting sentences. Typically, sentencing guidelines determine punishment based on the type of crime and the offender's criminal record. A judge may "depart" from the prescribed sentence only if the judge finds that mitigating or aggravating factors exist.

The intention of adopting guidelines was to provide consistency throughout a state, so that offenders who committed similar crimes were not punished more harshly by a judge in one part of a state and less harshly by a judge in another part of the state. The guidelines were also intended to address concerns about discrimination based on race, gender, and other protected characteristics, by providing an objective system for determining sentences.

Determinate and indeterminate sentences

A determinate sentence is a sentence for a set period of time. Officials have no discretion to reduce a determinate sentence for good behavior or due to mitigating factors. An example of a determinate sentence is a "three strikes" law that requires life imprisonment, without possibility of parole, after a third felony conviction. An indeterminate sentence consists of a maximum period of incarceration, with the possibility of parole or other early release. Some sentences are a combination between determinate and indeterminate. An example would be a requirement that an inmate serve a minimum number of years of his sentence, after which the inmate may be eligible for early release. Corrections officials often complain that determinate sentencing removes any incentive an inmate may have for good behavior, because the inmate cannot influence the length of his incarceration.

Concurrent and consecutive sentences

Concurrent sentences are sentences that an inmate is allowed to serve at the same time. The inmate's total sentence is the length of the longest sentence. Concurrent sentences may be imposed where the offender is sentenced for more than one crime arising out of the same incident. For example, a drunk driver who kills a pedestrian may be convicted of vehicular manslaughter, driving under the influence, and speeding, but may be allowed to serve the sentences for all three convictions simultaneously.

Consecutive sentences are sentences that the inmate must serve one after the other. The inmate's total sentence is the sum of all of the sentences added together. Consecutive sentences may be imposed where there is one criminal incident, but several victims. For example, an offender who murders three persons in a drive-by shooting may be convicted on three counts of murder and required to serve three sentences, consecutively.

Inmate classification

Inmate classification, or inmate custody category, refers to the custody requirements for an inmate based on his criminal record, number of years left on his sentence, behavior toward staff and other inmates, association with a security threat group (gang), history of escape attempts, and possible threats from others. In most states, classification of inmates is done according to objective guidelines.

Most institutions classify inmates as minimum, medium, and maximum security. Some institutions recognize a fourth custody level, "close custody," for inmates who are considered to pose a risk of violence toward others. An inmate's classification determines the type of facility in which he is confined, housing within the facility, and the programs he can participate in. For example, an inmate classified as maximum security will generally be sent to a maximum-security institution.

Protective custody

There are two types of protective custody in prisons. The first is the protected custody extended to federal witnesses who are incarcerated. This type of protective custody is similar to a regular witness protection program in that the goal is to protect the individual so he or she can provide testimony against another person. A federal prison may have an entire unit devoted to this type of custody. Inmates in federal witness protection generally have less restrictions and more privileges than they would experience under other levels of security.

The second type of protective custody is that given to inmates who have been threatened or harassed by other inmates. This type of custody is more restrictive because the goal is to protect the inmate from others.

"Good time"

"Good time" refers to credits an inmate may earn through good behavior while in prison. Good time provides an incentive for the inmate to behave well in prison. The credits shorten the time until the inmate is eligible for parole.

Not all inmates are eligible for good time. Inmates who commit certain offenses are not eligible. In some jurisdictions, most notably those with "three strikes" rules, repeat offenders are not eligible for good time. Some jurisdictions – those with determinate sentencing – do not recognize any good time.

Critics of good time complain that the reduction in time served is misleading to jurors who do the sentencing. A well-behaved inmate might serve one-third of his sentence. This has led to "truth in sentencing" laws, which require that jurors be informed of the effect of good time at the time they are deciding the sentence.

Honor blocks

An honor block is a block of cells for inmates who have maintained good behavior for a specified period of time. There may be other requirements for transfer to the honor block, such as having a prison job.

Inmates in honor blocks usually receive more privileges, such as better visitation and more freedom of movement. They may also have better facilities, such as larger cells and hot tap water inside the cell.

Placement in the honor block must be earned through good behavior and specifically requested by the inmate. The inmate must continue to earn the placement while in the honor block. Any disciplinary infraction can result return to a regular cell block.

A "count"

A "count" is a full head count of all inmates in a facility or in a particular unit of a facility. Counts are taken several times a day, usually at specified times. Typically, inmates are required to return to their cells for the count. An accurate count helps the facility ensure that no inmate has escaped or is in an unauthorized location. If an inmate does escape, his absence will be discovered by the next count. The count also gives officers an opportunity to see every inmate regularly to make sure that no inmate's physical status has changed dramatically. A formal count involves the entire facility. In addition, officers conduct informal counts at the beginning and end of each shift.

Constitutional rights of inmates

Convicted prisoners do not lose all of their constitutional rights. They do, however, lose some. They lose those rights that are inconsistent with incarceration, such as the right to liberty. In addition, they are not protected from prison regulations that have a "rational relationship" to legitimate penological interests. Legitimate penological interests include rehabilitation, deterrence of crime, and institutional security. If the prison can demonstrate a rational relationship between an institutional rule and these interests, the rule will be upheld, even if it impinges on an inmate's constitutional rights. Pretrial detainees – those who are in jail awaiting trial – also have the right not to be punished, because they have not yet been found guilty.

The First Amendment

The First Amendment guarantees freedom of expression. Freedom of expression encompasses four basic liberties: freedom of speech, religion, press, and assembly. Freedom of speech is the right to express one's views, as well as the right to receive the views of others. Freedom of religion is the right to practice one's own religious beliefs. Freedom of the press is the right of the media to publish as well as the right of citizens to communicate information to the media that is of public interest. Freedom of assembly – also called freedom of association – is the right of an individual to join others in a group and the right to associate with another person.

The First Amendment to the Constitution states that no law should be allowed to infringe on the freedoms of religion, speech, press, peaceable assembly, and petition. In order to retain the security of a correctional facility, it is often necessary to suspend First Amendment rights. Outside of correctional institutions, it must be demonstrated that the exercise of these rights is a "clear and present danger" before they can be curtailed. Correctional facilities have a much lower burden of proof in cases regarding the suspension of First Amendment rights.

Inmate mail: Courts divide inmate mail into two categories for First Amendment analysis: nonlegal and legal. As to nonlegal mail, courts distinguish between mere inspection, to search for contraband, and censorship, the actual withholding of mail. Prisons have broad discretion to inspect nonlegal inmate mail, if the search is necessary to serve legitimate penological interests. Censorship of nonlegal mail, on the other hand, raises free speech issues. The institution must demonstrate how censorship furthers legitimate penological interests. In addition, the institution must notify the inmate and the author of the censorship and provide an opportunity for review. Legal mail, by contrast, is absolutely protected. Mail between inmates and courts, attorneys, or their representatives may not be opened and searched for contraband unless the inmate is present.

Although there is not a specific law governing inbound and outbound mail of inmates, Supreme Court cases have demonstrated that certain material, such as racist or pornographic material, can be blocked from entry into a correctional facility. However, any time mail is blocked the prisoner must be notified and given a chance to protest. A prisoner's legal mail or mail from the media cannot be read by unauthorized individuals, though it must be opened in the presence of the prisoner and searched for contraband. Outbound mail is much less restricted, and is usually opened only when it is believed to contain information that threatens security or rehabilitation.

Inmate religious beliefs: The First Amendment protects inmates in their religious beliefs. This means, first, that a prison cannot force inmates to practice a particular religion or, for that matter, to practice any religion at all. Second, the prison cannot discriminate against or disparage an inmate for following his or her religious beliefs.

The more difficult question is the extent to which prisons must accommodate religious practices. Generally, courts require prisons to reasonably accommodate religious practices that do not conflict with legitimate penological interests. For example, a prison may have to accommodate the dietary restrictions of a Jewish inmate, but not the hair-length restrictions of a Native American inmate if the prison already restricted inmate hair length for security and health reasons.

Inmate access to the media: An institution may restrict media access to inmates if the restriction meets the four parts of the *Turner* test. If an institution permits media access, it may restrict the conditions of the access, such as barring face-to-face interviews.

There are two limits on the above. First, the restrictions may not be an "exaggerated response" to prison concerns. Second, the restrictions may not be based on the content of the inmate's speech. For example, a prison may not permit media access to inmates with positive comments about the institution, while restricting access to inmates with complaints.

31

Finally, the press does not have a right of access to any individual inmate. Such access would be greater than the media's right of access to citizens in the general population, and there is no basis for such greater access.

Inmate visitation: Inmate visitation involves the First Amendment right to freedom of association. The most significant outside relationships for most inmates are those with family and other visitors. Prison restrictions on contact visits have been upheld as constitutional. In the 2003 case of *Overton v. Bazzetta*, the Supreme Court upheld restrictions on the number and type of non-contact visits inmates could receive under Michigan rules. These rules limited visits by minors to the children and grandchildren of the inmate. Former inmates could visit only if related to the inmate. An inmate with two or more substance abuse violations could only have visits from lawyers and clergy. The court held that all of these restrictions were legitimate.

Inmate access to books, newspapers, magazines, and similar material: Citizens in the general population have a First Amendment right of access to printed media. Inmates have that same right, but it can be curtailed by the institution if the *Turner* test is satisfied. The Supreme Court recently held that a prison could cut off inmate access to secular (non-religious) newspapers and periodicals for inmates who were assigned to a high-security unit. Prison officials justified the rule on the ground that it provided an incentive for inmates to comply with prison rules.

Most prisons ban hard-core pornography, child pornography, sadomasochistic pornography, literature from hate groups, and weapons manuals, all on the ground that they create security threats. Courts will generally defer to prison officials' judgment on these matters. Similarly, the Supreme Court upheld a ban on hardback books not mailed directly from the publisher. The prison argued that the rule addressed a security threat.

The Fourth Amendment

The Fourth Amendment protects citizens against unreasonable searches and seizures by the government. The three elements of a Fourth Amendment claim are: (1) reasonableness; (2) justification; and (3) expectation of privacy.

Reasonableness: The key to any Fourth Amendment claim is whether the government's actions were "reasonable." Courts will look at whether a search was "justified at its inception," as opposed to being justified because contraband was in fact located, and reasonable in the way that the search is conducted.

As to privacy, courts will look at whether the individual has a reasonable expectation of privacy in the area searched, whether that is the individual's body, his clothing, his possessions, or his living space. Even if an individual has a reasonable expectation of privacy, the individual can waive his rights by consenting to the search. Thus, a frequent question in privacy cases is whether the individual voluntarily consented. Consent to premises by a third party, such as a cellmate, is effective if that party had common authority of the premises.

Searches: Inmates have little Fourth Amendment protection. Prison officials are free to search an inmate's possessions and living quarters, with or without reasonable cause. Random, "shake down" searches have been upheld by the courts. The Supreme Court has concluded that an inmate has no reasonable expectation of privacy in his cell or its contents. However, any searches must be conducted pursuant to a valid prison regulation and may not be for purposes of harassment or wanton destruction of the inmate's property.

The rules for inspection of an inmate's person are more restrictive. Generally, the greater the intrusive of the search, the greater the reason must be for conducting the search. A visual search of a fully clothed inmate is minimally invasive and so requires little or no justification. On the other hand, a body cavity search must in most cases be based on reasonable suspicion that the inmate is hiding contraband.

In order for an officer's suspicion to be considered reasonable by a court, it must be based on a combination of fact and professional judgment. In other words, there must be a specific fact that arouses the suspicion, and the suspicion must be focused on a particular individual or group rather than on the prison population as a whole. The courts have rules that anonymous tips do not constitute a fact that can justify invasive searches. Whenever a full body search or strip search is performed, the rationale must be documented.

Cross-gender searches: Courts balance the intrusiveness of the search against the justification for the search, and then determine whether the gender of the officer is a factor. They also factor in female officers' equal employment rights.

Visual: Visual inspection of a fully-clothed inmate is permissible by either gender of officer. A female officer may observe male inmates who are not clothed – such as in the shower – but it is less clear whether a male officer may observe female inmates under the same situations.

Pat-down searches: Pat down searches of fully-clothed inmates, conducted pursuant to established rules and procedures, are usually permissible by either gender, even if the anal and genital area is involved.

Strip/body cavity searches: Strip searches and body cavity searches are usually permitted where the inmate is male and the officer is female. Courts are hesitant to these intrusive searches of female inmates by male officers, however.

The courts have sanctioned both males and females to act as prison guards over both male and female prison populations. However, it is becoming increasingly clear that female prisoners have greater privacy needs. Most female prisoners are unwilling to be naked in front of male prison guards, though male prisoners are not unwilling to be naked in front of female guards. Searches also provide opportunity for conflict. Searches should only be performed by prisoners of the same sex unless there is an emergency.

The Fifth Amendment

The three elements of the Fifth Amendment that arise in the corrections context are the prohibitions against double jeopardy, self-incrimination, and punishment without due process of law.

Double jeopardy is putting a defendant "in jeopardy" more than once for the same offense. This may include a second prosecution for the same offense, after either acquittal or conviction. It may also encompass multiple punishments for the same offense. The two most common double jeopardy claims are prison discipline and correction of administrative mistakes.

The first situation arises when an inmate who commits an offense while in prison faces criminal charges and administrative discipline for the offense. Inmates argue that this violates the double jeopardy clause because they are being punished twice for the same offense. Courts reject these claims because the double jeopardy clause applies only to criminal punishments. Institutional discipline is not the same as criminal punishment.

The second situation arises when the institution or criminal justice system makes a mistake regarding an inmate, such as erroneously releasing an inmate early, then reincarcerating him when the mistake is discovered. Other examples are mistakes in calculating sentences or good time. Courts have held that correction of clerical mistakes is not a criminal prosecution or punishment.

Self-incrimination, another element of the Fifth Amendment, is the privilege not to have to testify against oneself if the testimony might result in criminal sanctions, including fines and other penalties. This privilege is not available if the government grants the witness immunity from prosecution. The due process clause of the Fifth Amendment prohibits the government from depriving a person of life, liberty, or property without due process of law.

Treatment programs

An inmate's participation in a treatment program violates the Fifth Amendment if: (1) the inmate's case is on appeal; and (2) the inmate's participation is coerced.

Inmates complain that participation in certain treatment programs, such as for sex offenders, constitutes an admission of guilt. This is important only if an inmate is appealing his conviction. Once all appeals have been exhausted, the issue of self-incrimination is moot.

In *McKune v. Lile*, the Supreme Court held that a prison does not violate the Fifth Amendment by removing certain incentives – such as preferred housing – if an inmate refuses participation, even if there are negative consequences to the inmate. This is because the Fifth Amendment does not prohibit all self-incrimination, just *compelled* self-incrimination. Therefore, an institution may offer incentives to participate. An institution cannot coerce or force an inmate to participate.

Miranda warnings

An inmate is entitled to a *Miranda* warning if: (1) he is being interrogated; (2) about a potential criminal matter. In *Miranda v. Arizona*, the Supreme Court held that, due to the coercive nature of custodial interrogation, a suspect must be informed of his rights. Inmates are in a custodial situation, but an inmate is not entitled to a *Miranda* warning every time he is questioned about his conduct.

Courts look at the conditions of the confession. Admissions to corrections staff under ordinary prison conditions are not "interrogations." If the inmate is separated from the rest of the population and interviewed under coercive conditions not normally experienced in prison, a *Miranda* warning may be required. Similarly, confessions to cellmate informants, even if they are undercover officers, are admissible if they are not coerced. Finally, a *Miranda* warning is not required for disciplinary actions, only criminal charges.

The Sixth Amendment

There are three elements of the right to effective assistance of counsel in the Sixth Amendment. The three elements are: (1) access; (2) privacy; (3) and effective assistance.

- Access: An inmate has a right of access to counsel. This right is not limited to assistance with criminal charges. It encompasses any legal counseling.
- Privacy: An inmate has a right to privacy of communication with counsel. As a general rule, prison staff may not read an inmate's correspondence with his attorney or listen to his conversations with his attorney. Incidental monitoring may not violate the Sixth Amendment if information is not shared with the prosecution. Systematic monitoring would violate the Sixth Amendment, even if information is not shared with the prosecution, because of the chilling (self-censoring) effect it could have on inmate-counsel communications.
- Effective Assistance: For effective assistance of counsel, the inmate and attorney must be permitted to form a relationship. Accordingly, the prison may not arbitrarily limit the inmate's access to legal counsel.

The Eighth Amendment

The Eighth Amendment prohibits cruel and unusual punishment. The courts system is in a continuous process of determining what constitutes cruel and unusual punishment. Some of the basic guidelines suggest that a punishment can be considered cruel and unusual if it: shocks the conscience of the court; violates the evolving standards of decency of a civilized society; is disproportionate to the offense; and entails the wanton and unnecessary infliction of pain. To prevail on a claim that the conditions of confinement violate this prohibition, an inmate must demonstrate that: (1) prison officials were deliberately indifferent to: (2) unconstitutional conditions of confinement.

As to conditions of confinement, inmates are entitled to "the minimum civilized measure of life's necessities." This includes essential food, medical care, and sanitation, as well as protection from harm by other inmates and from excessive force. In evaluating the conditions of confinement, courts will look at individual factors alone and in combination, to determine the "totality of circumstances." Overcrowding is not a violation in itself, but the effects of overcrowding on health, sanitation, and safety may be a violation due to their combined impact.

The courts system may rule on the conditions of confinement in cases where the conditions are thought to lack safety or some other basic human need. The human needs that must be provided in any correctional setting are as follows: adequate exercise; nutritional diet; clothing appropriate to the climate conditions of the institution; shelter (including plumbing, ventilation; and climate control); sanitation; medical care; and reasonable safety.

Excessive force: Force is excessive if it was not justified by a legitimate penological purpose or if it was disproportionate to the purpose. Although officials may use force to restore and maintain discipline, they may not use it maliciously and sadistically.

Justified: In determining whether force was justified, courts look at the extent of the risk to inmates and staff. They also look at whether efforts were made to reduce the risk through other methods before using force. Sexual contact between a prison official and an inmate is never justified, even if it was "consensual," because of the imbalance of power.

Proportionate: In determining whether force was proportionate, courts look at the immediacy and seriousness of the threat. Force used after the threat has passed is rarely justified. Courts will also consider the extent of the inmate's injuries. An inmate need not show a serious or permanent physical injury, however.

There are three types of records that are especially important in determining whether excessive force has been used:

- Videotapes: perhaps the most effective way of describing the situation to a judge or jury
- Incident reports: detailed summaries composed after any situation in which force was required; these reports should include a description of the force used as well as the justification for the force
- Medical records: in most cases, inmates should be examined after force has been used; inmates should be treated for any injuries sustained as a result of force

A correctional officer should be sure to abide by any institutional, state, or federal policies regarding the use of force. Force should only be used in situations where all other means have been exhausted, and should never be considered an appropriate means of punishment. Any time force is used, it must be documented and submitted for review by supervisors. Finally, if a court is required to examine the use of force, it will do so from the point of view of the correctional officer.

Liability: The two conditions under which an officer may be liable for the excessive force of another officer are: (1) failure to intervene; or (2) supervisor liability.

- Failure to Intervene: An officer is liable for the excessive force of another if the officer was present when the force was being used and he failed to intervene to stop it. In such cases, courts apply the "deliberate indifference" standard, rather than "malicious and sadistic."
- Supervisory Liability: A supervisor is liable for the excessive force of a subordinate if the supervisor was deliberately indifferent to the risk of a violation. This may arise, for example, where excessive force is regularly used in an institution, with the knowledge of a supervisor, the supervisor fails to take corrective action, and an inmate is seriously injured.

Failure to protect an inmate from another inmate: The four elements of a claim of this nature are:

- Substantial Risk of Serious Harm: A strong likelihood, rather than a mere possibility, that the inmate would suffer serious harm. There is no bright line rule for when an injury is "serious," but minor injuries probably are not enough.
- Official Knew of Risk: The official must have known there was risk to the specific inmate, to a group to which the inmate belong, or within the prison in general. Knowledge may arise because the official was specifically told of the risk or because the risk was obvious.
- Unreasonable Failure to Respond: The official must have failed to reasonably respond to the risk. This does not mean the official must eliminate the risk in every case, just that the official made good faith efforts to address the risk.
- Causation: There must be a connection between the official's failure to respond and the assault.

Failure-to-protect claims: The six most common failure-to-protect claims are:

- Unusually vulnerable inmates: Officials failed to take reasonable steps to protect an inmate who was a likely target of assault. Likely targets include informants, the mentally ill, inmates who are smaller, and those known as homosexuals.
- Unusually dangerous inmates: Officials failed to properly classify and isolate unusually dangerous inmates, especially inmates with a history of violence behind bars.
- Attacker threatened victim: Officials failed to reasonably protect an inmate who was threatened.
- Failure to intervene: Officials witnessed an attack, but failed to take reasonable steps to stop it. Officials need not, however, endanger their own safety.
- Overcrowding and Understaffing: These conditions do not, alone, violate the constitution. If, however, they lead to more violence, then they may give rise to a failure- to-protect claim.

"Deliberate indifference"

Occasionally, a prisoner will claim that his or her rights under the Eighth Amendment have been violated by incompetent or negligent medical care or safety care. For instance, an officer can be charged with deliberate indifference if he or she does not allow a prisoner to visit a doctor. The medical staff can be held responsible if the care they provide is inadequate or indifferent to serious medical needs. Another scenario in which an institution or individual can be charged with negligence or deliberate indifference is when a preexisting medical condition is not considered when establishing a prisoner's living conditions.

A prison official displays deliberate indifference if he had actual knowledge of a serious risk of substantial injury and unreasonably failed to take action to correct the problem.

- Actual knowledge: The official must have had actual knowledge of the conditions and that the conditions posed a substantial risk of serious injury to inmates. Knowledge can be inferred if the conditions are longstanding, pervasive, well-documented, or expressly noted. An inmate need not show an intent to harm, but must show more than mere negligence.
- Unreasonable failure to act: A prison official must make a good faith effort to investigate the problem and fix it. In deciding whether an official's response was reasonable, courts look at the information he possessed at the time, the practical limitations of his position, and any alternative courses of action that would have been apparent to an official in his position. Cost is not a defense.

The Fourteenth Amendment

The Fourteenth Amendment to the Constitution declares that the state should not "deprive any person of life, liberty, or property without due process of law." Also, it declares that no state should "deny to any person within its jurisdiction the equal protection of the laws." In other words, a person must be given due process before they are incarcerated. Also, no person should be denied the rights to defend themselves accorded by law. Although this due process law is directed at the state governments, there is a similar provision applying to the federal government in the Fifth Amendment.

The steps of due process when a serious sanction is threatened are as follows:
- There is a hearing at which the inmate has a right to be present.
- The inmate is given notice of the charges against him or her at least 24 hours before the hearing.
- The inmate is given the opportunity to call witnesses and present evidence on his or her own behalf.
- Although the inmate does not have a right to counsel, he or she does have a right to assistance if he or she is illiterate or otherwise prevented from preparing for the hearing.
- The inmate has the right to an impartial tribunal, excluding any individual who was involved in the alleged infraction
- The tribunal is required to record its findings, ruling, and rationale in writing.

Due process policies for disciplinary actions: court cases
- *Wolff v. McDonnell* (1974): a hearing is required when good time is forfeited due to misbehavior; also, a hearing is required when an inmate faces a term of segregation due to misbehavior
- *Sandin v. Conner* (1995): the terms of the *Wolff* decision were declared to be inapplicable to cases in which the disciplinary hearing would result in less than 30 days of segregation; unless the possible sanction imposes "atypical deprivation in relation to a normal prison life," a hearing is not necessary. Cases in which an inmate is medicated without consent or is committed to a mental institution require a due process hearing.

Procedural due process vs. substantive due process: Substantive due process is primarily concerned with the action that was taken, while procedural due process focuses on the way that action was performed. The courts insist that the corrections system abide by procedural due process so that the rights of prisoners will not be infringed upon. An issue of substantive due process concerns whether the institution has the right to do something in the first place, even when all of the necessary procedures are followed.

The Religious Land Use and Institutionalized Persons Act (RLUIPA)

Passed in 2000, the RLUIPA prohibits the government from imposing a substantial burden on the religious exercise of an inmate unless the burden: (1) furthers a "compelling governmental interest"; and (2) is the "least restrictive means" of furthering that interest.

The RLUIPA applies to individual acts burdening an inmate's religious exercise, and to rules of "general applicability" that have the effect, intentional or unintentional, of burdening an inmate's religious exercise.

The Act defines "religious exercise" broadly. An inmate need not be a member of a recognized religion. If the inmate is a member of a recognized religion, the exercise is protected even if it is not required by that religion.

In the 2005 case of *Cutter v. Wilkinson*, the Supreme Court held that the law is not unconstitutional, even if it results in more favorable treatment of inmate religious practices than other inmate practices.

The *Turner* test

The *Turner* test was developed by the Supreme Court in 1987 in the case of *Turner v. Safley*. This test is used to determine the constitutionality of prison regulations that infringe on an inmate's First Amendment rights. There are four parts to the test:
- Whether there is a valid, rational connection between the regulation and a legitimate penological interest;
- Whether the inmate has access to alternative means of exercising his rights;
- Whether accommodation of the inmate's rights would have a "ripple effect" on the rest of the prison; and
- Whether there is a ready alternative to the regulation that would accommodate the inmate's rights at minimal cost to penological interests.

In the *Turner* case, the Supreme Court upheld Ohio regulations restricting correspondence between inmates at different facilities. However, the court also struck down a requirement that the warden give permission for inmate marriages.

A Son of Sam law

A Son of Sam law prevents an inmate from profiting from his crimes through books and other media deals. These laws require the proceeds to go to the victim(s) of the crime. Approximately 40 states have adopted such laws.

In 1991, the Supreme Court struck down New York's Son of Sam law as overbroad and in violation of inmates' free speech rights under the First Amendment. The laws in many other states have either been struck down or are rarely invoked. As a result, the trend is away from mandatory forfeiture laws.

Crime victims may still access proceeds from media deals through civil lawsuits. As in the OJ Simpson case, the victim's family can always sue the inmate and collect any damages awarded from the inmate's assets. These assets would include proceeds from media deals.

Prison Rape Elimination Commission

Passed in 2003, the Prison Rape Elimination Act (PREA) created the Prison Rape Elimination Commission. The Commission's three duties are:
- Study: The Commission is charged with conducting a two-year study of the policies and practices of corrections facilities for the prevention, detection, and punishment of prison rape regardless of whether committed by other inmates or by prison officials. The study must encompass the psychological and physical effects of prison rape, within the prison and in the community.
- Standards: The Commission must develop national standards, with the stated goal of making elimination of prison rape a top priority in every institution
- Report: At the end of its study, the Commission must report its findings and recommendations to Congress and the President.

Right to medical care

Inmates have a constitutional right to medical care that those in the outside world do not. The Supreme Court has held that failure to provide medical care can cause pain and suffering, which does not serve a penological purpose. Moreover, because they are incarcerated, inmates do not have the ability to seek out treatment on their own. They also may not be able to take recommended actions to prevent illness or injury, such as avoiding secondhand smoke, following a modified diet, or having regular dental cleanings.

The obligation to provide medical care may extend after release. Prison officials have a duty to continue to provide medical care after release until the offender can secure treatment on his own. For example, officials should provide an inmate who has a chronic condition with sufficient medicine to allow time for the offender to consult a provider to obtain a prescription.

Medical care claims

The four elements of a medical care claim are:
- <u>Serious medical need:</u> It must be life threatening, progressive (getting steadily worse), or very painful.
- <u>Official knowledge:</u> The official must be aware of the problem and any special threat the problem poses for the individual. For example, the common cold is not serious for the average adult, but can be very serious for someone with AIDS.
- <u>Unreasonable failure to provide treatment:</u> The official has a duty to take reasonable steps to obtain medical care. An official may not refuse to provide medically-adequate care because of cost. With infectious diseases, officials have a duty to obtain treatment to assist the individual *and* to prevent the spread of the infection to others.
- <u>Causation:</u> The inmate must show that the official's actions caused the inmate further injury, or unnecessary and wanton pain and suffering.

Medical care claims take three forms: (1) denial or delay of access to care; (3) inadequate care; or (3) interference with prescribed treatment.
- <u>Denial or delay:</u> An inmate may assert that an officer refused to allow him to see medical staff. An officer should not act as gatekeeper to medical staff unless he or she has been properly trained. Similarly, a member of the medical staff without specialized training should not deny an inmate access to a specialist. A delay in providing treatment may be unconstitutional if it is medically unjustified and clearly likely to make the inmate's condition worse.
- <u>Inadequate care:</u> Inmates do not have a right to choose their care, and medical malpractice (negligence) is not unconstitutional. However, grossly incompetent or inadequate care may violate inmates' rights.
- <u>Interference:</u> Once medical staff prescribes treatment, corrections staff may not interfere with the treatment.

Medical care lawsuits

To be liable for failure to provide medical care, a supervisor or government must have established or tolerated a deliberately indifferent policy or custom. Claims against supervisors and governments are called *systemic* claims, because they challenge the system, rather than the actions of individuals.

There are three common systemic claims for failure to provide medical care. The first is failure to provide adequate medical staff. This includes both quantity of staff – sufficient to treat inmates' medical needs -- and quality of staff – staff with appropriate qualifications. Second is failure to provide adequate medical facilities, either at the prison or at an outside location. The third claim is for failure to provide access to staff and facilities – essentially, failure to screen for short- and long-term medical problems and failure to have a workable sick call policy.

HIV and AIDS

An inmate is four times as likely as a person in the general population to be infected with HIV – human immunodeficiency virus. HIV is a virus that attacks the body's immune system. AIDS -- acquired immunodeficiency syndrome – is the condition that results when HIV weakens the immune system. The body is then vulnerable to opportunistic infections, such as pneumonia. A person infected with HIV may have no symptoms. A person with AIDS may be very sick.

HIV is spread through contact with blood, semen, vaginal fluid, or breast milk. It is not spread through contact with saliva or other casual contact. AIDS is a syndrome and is not itself contagious, although any infection may be contagious.

The progress of HIV can be slowed using protease inhibitors and other medications. AIDS is not itself treatable, but the infection may be treated or managed.

STDs

The most common sexually transmitted diseases (STDs) in the inmate population are syphilis, gonorrhea, chlamydia, and herpes. These infections may or may not be symptomatic. All are treatable. If they are not treated, however, they may have long-term impact on the inmate's fertility and may lead to more serious problems, such as cancer.

Inmates are a high-risk population for STDs, which are communicated through unprotected sexual activity and intravenous drug use. Infected inmates pose a risk to other inmates and to their partners upon release.

Health authorities see the inmate and detainee population as an opportunity to address the spread of STDs. Health authorities advocate routine screening and treatment of all arrestees, detainees, and convicts. They also advocate educational programs targeted at this risk group.

Tuberculosis

Prison inmates make up one of the five high-risk groups for tuberculosis (TB). TB is caused by a bacterium that attacks the lungs, throat, brain, and spine. Symptoms include fever, chills, coughing, and spitting up blood.

Most people with TB do not have symptoms. This is called *latent* TB. Latent TB is detected through a skin test. Latent TB is not contagious. TB that is symptomatic is called *active* TB. A person with active TB is highly contagious. The disease is spread through the air when the infected person coughs or sneezes. Because active TB is so contagious, an infected person must be isolated to prevent its spread to the rest of the population.

A person with latent TB can be treated to reduce the risk of an active infection. A person with active TB must be treated with antibiotics over a long period of time – 12 months or more.

Diabetes

An estimated 5% of inmates have diabetes. Diabetes is a disorder in the body's ability to metabolize food due to shortage of insulin, resulting in high blood sugar. Diabetes can damage the heart, kidney, and nerves, as well as the body's ability to heal itself. A person may develop diabetes as a child or as an adult.

Diabetes is not contagious. There is a strong genetic link, but some people who develop diabetes have no history of the disease in their family. Obesity is a risk factor for diabetes. Also, racial minorities, including Hispanics, African Americans, Asian Americans, and Pacific Islanders, are at higher risk for diabetes.

Diabetes is treated through the management of blood sugar levels. This may involve insulin injections, dietary restrictions, and an exercise program. Inmates with diabetes require long-term medical treatment, with an emphasis on self-management.

Epilepsy

Epilepsy is a seizure disorder, caused by uncontrolled electrical activity in the brain. Some seizures involve loss of consciousness, such as *grand mal* seizures. Other seizures have isolated effects. For example, a seizure may affect a person's sense of smell, sound, or taste. Most seizures last less than a minute.

Epilepsy has many causes. One common cause is a head or brain injury, such as from head trauma, a brain infection, or a brain tumor. Epilepsy is more common among inmates than among the general population. Experts speculate that inmates are more likely to have suffered head injuries. Some argue that epileptics are more like to be incarcerated because one type of the disorder – temporal lobe epilepsy – is associated with violent tendencies.

Epilepsy is treated with anti-seizure medication. Even with medication, some people will continue to have seizures, although their seizures may be less frequent or less severe.

Disability and the ADA

The Americans with Disabilities Act (ADA) outlaws discrimination on the basis of disability in employment, accommodations, telecommunications, transportation, and public facilities. Inmates and correctional officers alike enjoy the rights provided by this act. According to the ADA, a disability is any physical or mental impairment that would limit one or more life activities of a person. Individuals may also be considered disabled if they have a history of such impairment, or are regarded by others as having such an impairment.

The Americans with Disabilities Act (ADA) defines a disability as a mental or physical impairment that significantly limits a major life activity. A person is also considered disabled if he has a past record of disability or if someone perceives him as having a disability. Examples of disabilities include paralysis, blindness, deafness, clinical depression, and intellectual disability.

Disabled inmates have three basic rights. First, they are protected from discrimination. Prison officials cannot treat a disabled inmate differently because of his disability. Second, a disabled inmate is entitled to accessible facilities. Third, inmates are entitled to reasonable accommodation. Prison officials must include disabled inmates in prison programs and activities, unless that would fundamentally change a program or activity or cause the prison "undue hardship."

Pregnant inmates

The three basic rights of pregnant inmates are prenatal care, abortion, and medical care during labor. Prenatal care includes regular visits to a qualified provider, appropriate nutrition, and prenatal vitamins. Inmates have the right to an abortion until the fetus is capable of sustaining itself outside the womb, or if the life of the mother is in danger or in the case of rape. Federal funds may not be used to pay for an abortion, but they may be used to transport an inmate to an abortion provider.

Inmates have the right to medical care during labor. Due to recent controversy, most institutions will not shackle an inmate during labor unless there is a risk to staff, the baby, or the inmate herself. Inmates do not have the right to keep their babies with them after birth.

Suicide

The three groups of inmates that are at risk for suicide are the mentally ill, those withdrawing from drugs and alcohol, and those experiencing trauma from arrest or incarceration.

Suicide is the leading cause of death among inmates, with a suicide rate ten times higher than the general population. This has been attributed to three factors: a high rate of mental illness in the inmate population, enforced withdrawal from drugs and alcohol upon incarceration, and traumatic reaction to incarceration. A major difference between these three is in timing. Those who commit suicide in reaction to the trauma of arrest or incarceration are most likely to act within the first 24 hours. Those who commit suicide due to drug or alcohol withdrawal are most likely to act during the withdrawal period. The mentally ill, on the other hand, may act at any time, including months after arrest or incarceration.

The three most common claims in inmate suicide cases are: (1) failure to identify; (2) failure to monitor; and (3) failure to respond. Failure to identify includes failure to recognize that an inmate is a suicide risk. It also encompasses failure to communicate concerns to other officers, such as during shift changes, or to other institutions upon transfer. Failure to monitor includes failure to make rounds or failure of technological monitoring. Because of monitoring challenges, some institutions will use inmate monitors. Failure to respond includes the situation where staff is not trained to handle medical emergencies. These claims may also encompass failure to address vehicles for suicide. For example, removing implements from the inmate or blocking access to upper level "jumping off" points.

Viral hepatitis

The three most common types of viral hepatitis are A (HAV), B (HBV), and C (HCV). HAV is transmitted through the oral-fecal route. It is contracted through oral contact with feces, raw seafood, or contaminated food or water. HAV causes acute illness, but the body is capable of fighting the virus with appropriate medical treatment.

HBV is transmitted through blood, such as through transfusions (in third world countries), tattoos, or needle-sharing. It causes acute illness and, in some cases, chronic infection. Acute HBV is treated with bed rest and medication. Some cases of chronic respond to medication.

HCV is transmitted through blood, as with HBV. It causes chronic illness, but may be asymptomatic for 10 years or long. HCV causes tremendous damage and is usually fatal. Some cases of HCV respond to interferon. Vaccines are available for HAV and HBV, but not for HCV.

Asthma

Asthma is inflammation of the lungs. It makes breathing difficult and can even result in death. Symptoms include characteristic wheezing, coughing, and shortness of breath.

Asthma is not a contagious disease. It varies in severity. Some people have regular problems while others have only occasional problems. Asthma attacks are brought on by physical and environmental "triggers," usually allergies or respiratory illness. These triggers vary from person to person. For some, animal allergies will provoke an asthma attack. For others, cigarette smoke may be a trigger.

Asthma cannot be cured, but it can be managed through medications and environmental changes. Medications are classified as "relief" – used to treat symptoms during an attack – and preventative – used to reduce inflammation in the lungs. Relief medications are vital during an attack to prevent serious injury or death.

Drug abuse

The five classes of commonly abused drugs are: opiates and narcotics; central nervous system (CNS) stimulants; CNS depressants; hallucinogens; and tetrahydrocannabinols.
- Opiates and narcotics: These are painkillers that produce a euphoric effect. Opiates include heroin, opium, codeine, morphine, and oxycontin.
- CNS stimulants: These drugs produce a stimulating effect. Stimulants include cocaine and meth (methamphetamine), as well as nicotine and caffeine.
- CNS depressants: These drugs produce a soothing, anti-anxiety effect. Depressants include barbiturates (such as pentobarbital), benzodiazepine (such as Xanax and valium), and alcohol.
- Hallucinogens: These drugs produce hallucinations. They include LSD, PCP (angel dust), and mescaline.
- Tetrahydrocannabinols (THC): THC drugs produce a relaxing effect. They include marijuana and hashish.

Personality disorders

A personality disorder is a form of mental illness characterized by long-term behavioral and thought patterns. The Diagnostic and Statistical Manual of Mental Disorders, Fourth Edition, Text Revision (DSM-IV-TR) lists ten personality disorders, grouped into three classes. The three classes are:
- Class A: odd or eccentric. This group includes paranoid and schizoid personality types. (A schizoid personality is not the same as the mental illness schizophrenia.)
- Class B: dramatic, emotional, or erratic. This group includes borderline, antisocial, histrionic, and narcissistic personality types.
- Class C: anxious or fearful. This group includes the following: avoidant, dependent, and obsessive-compulsive personality types. (Obsessive-compulsive personality is not the same as obsessive-compulsive disorder.)

The DSM-IV-TR also lists behavioral patterns that are not classified as personality disorders, including passive-aggressiveness and self-defeating behavior.

Schizophrenia

Schizophrenia is a psychotic disorder characterized by disorganized thoughts, hallucinations, and impaired psychosocial skills. Management of schizophrenia requires a long-term, multidisciplinary treatment plan to address biological, interpersonal, cultural, and social needs.

Special considerations in the corrections setting include noncompliance, continuity of care, discharge planning, and psychosocial interventions. Noncompliance is a significant problem with schizophrenia. Patients may discontinue medication or fail to attend medical appointments, often with disastrous consequences. Along the same lines, continuity of care and discharge planning are important for inmates with schizophrenia. Detailed records and other communications are vital.

Finally, psychosocial interventions can minimize acute psychotic episodes and reinforce appropriate behaviors. Stressors for schizophrenics include periods of isolation, lack of structure, and stigmatization. It is important that schizophrenics have social interaction, to reality-test their perceptions. Schizophrenics respond well to positive reinforcement, such as privileges in the yard or priority in the dining hall.

Mental health treatment

Corrections officials must take reasonable steps to address the serious mental health issues of inmates. Unfortunately, mental health problems are very difficult to diagnose and there is no universally accepted definition of mental illness. If an official has knowledge of a serious problem, however, he may not be deliberately indifferent to the problem. Once a problem is identified, treatment should be made available to the inmate. Problems arise where the inmate refuses treatment, particularly medication.

The Supreme Court has held that an inmate may be forced to use anti-psychotic medication if: (1) the inmate presents a danger to himself or others; and (2) the medication is in his medical interest. Most institutions limit the administration of medication to court-ordered situations and emergencies. First, the institution will consider less restrictive alternatives. Even then, the medication will be administered in the lowest effective dose.

Elderly and terminally ill inmates

The average age of inmates is increasing faster than the overall prison population. The primary reason for this is longer sentences: truth-in-sentencing laws, determinate sentencing, and three-strikes laws. This means more inmates will live out their lives in prison.

There are two basic approaches for dealing with the end-of-life issues for elderly and other inmates: release or services. Most states and the Bureau of Prisons have mechanisms for early release of terminal of elderly patients. These include commutation or reduction of sentences, administrative leave, and furlough.

The other approach is to provide end-of-life services. Some states have units that are reserved for elderly inmates. Others provide for palliative (pain and disease management) care. A growing number of institutions are implementing hospice programs where the focus is on making the inmate comfortable.

Dental care

The inmate population is at high risk for dental problems. Most inmates come from "dentally illiterate" communities. Moreover, serious dental problems are associated with certain criminal activities, such as methamphetamine use.

Inmates have a constitutional right to treatment of cavities and similar problems that may become worse and cause undue pain. Inmates do not have a constitutional right to preventative dental care, such as routine cleanings, although many institutions provide such care. Similarly, they do not have the right to cosmetic procedures.

Inmates have the right to dental hygiene items, such as toothbrushes and toothpaste. Special toothbrushes and dental floss are manufactured for inmates that pose a lower security risk than conventional supplies. Health authorities view the period of incarceration as an opportunity. The National Commission on Correctional Health Care mandates dental education and oral-hygiene instruction for all inmates.

Bloodborne pathogens (BBP) programs

BBPs are diseases spread through contact with blood and other potentially infectious bodily fluids, including saliva, semen, mucous, and urine. A BBP program consists of three elements: (1) pre-exposure measures; (3) procedures to minimize exposure risk; and (4) post-exposure prophylaxis.

Pre-exposure measures consist of training and optional hepatitis B vaccination. Training must be provided upon hire and then repeated annually. The HBV vaccination must be offered to all employees, but an employee may decline. Procedures to minimize exposure risk include equipment and workplace practices. Workplace practices include universal precautions, which call for treating all blood and other potentially infectious material as if it is infected. Equipment consists primarily of barriers, such as personal protective equipment (PPE). Post-exposure prophylaxis consists of baseline testing of the employee, such as testing for HIV, HBV, and TB, testing of the source individual, and follow-up testing and treatment of the employee.

Fee-for-service programs

A number of agencies charge inmates a co-payment, typically less than $10, for routine medical visits. The funds come from the inmate's trust account. The revenues produced by these programs are insignificant relative to the cost of providing inmate medical care. Proponents argue that these programs reduce abuse of sick call and teach fiscal responsibility.

The NCCHC opposes fee-for-service programs on the grounds that they impede access to care. Nonetheless, inmate lawsuits challenging these programs have not been successful.

Because the constitution guarantees medical care, fee-for-service programs cannot be used to deny adequate medical care. Services must be provided even if there are insufficient funds in an inmate's trust account. Moreover, NCCHC recommends that institutions apply the fee only to services initiated by the inmate. NCCHC recommends exceptions to the fee for emergencies (life threatening illnesses or injuries), routine screenings, follow-up visits, referrals to specialists, lab work, and x-rays.

Civil rights law suits

There are two basic kinds of civil rights claim regularly brought against correctional institutions. In the first, the plaintiff alleges that the policies or procedures of the institution infringe upon his or her rights. In the second, the plaintiff alleges that an officer of the correctional facility failed to act in accordance with the policies and procedures of the institution, and thereby infringed upon the plaintiff's civil rights. For a correctional officer, the best defense against the latter suit is to learn and abide by the policies of the institution. The first kind of claim will only affect the career of an individual officer insofar as it affects the function of the institution as a whole.

Courts play in the judicial system

As regards the correctional system, the courts seek to protect the rights of prisoners while making sure that officers of the law are protected. One of the major issues addressed by the court system is what constitutes "cruel and unusual punishment." In some cases, the court system is unable to achieve a clear ruling, and so correctional institutions are left to interpret the law as they see fit.

The Supreme Court

There are three eras of the Supreme Court's relationship with corrections in the United States: Hands-Off, Hands-On, and One Hand On, One Hand Off.

Until the 1960s, the Supreme Court took a hands-off approach, rejecting prisoner lawsuits regarding conditions of confinement. The justification for this approach was that corrections officials knew more about running prisons than did judges. Moreover, society showed little concern for prison conditions.

During the 1960s and 1970s, the Supreme Court focused on civil rights, deciding landmark desegregation (Brown v. Board of Education) and suspect rights cases (Miranda v. Arizona). The court began to take a hands-on approach to prison conditions, leading to recognition that even inmates have some constitutional rights.

More recently, the court has taken a One Hand Off, One Hand On approach. The court recognizes that the constitution guarantees certain minimum standards for prison conditions. Out of deference to prison officials, however, the court has placed the burden on inmates to prove violations.

The Prison Litigation Reform Act

The Prison Litigation Reform Act, passed in the 1990s, aimed to stem the flood of lawsuits in which inmates claimed violations of their civil rights. This act made it more difficult for prisoners to file frivolous suits, basically by forcing them to pay for their own legal fees. Also, any prisoner who had three suits dismissed was banned from filing any more without being in imminent danger and paying the entire filing fee up front. The act also encourages prisoners to try settling their complaints through administrative channels before entering the courts system.

Inmate litigation

There are three general categories of inmate litigation: tort suits, habeas corpus actions, and civil rights actions. A tort suit is filed in cases where an inmate claims to have been damaged or endangered because of the negligence of someone else. A habeas corpus action is filed when the inmate questions the constitutionality of his or her being in prison. This kind of case typically hinges on whether a certain kind of incarceration is determined to be cruel and unusual. Finally, a civil rights action is brought when an inmate asserts that his or her constitutional rights have been violated by the conditions or policies of the institution, or by the actions of an officer.

If it is determined that an inmate's rights have been violated, he or she may receive either an injunction or damages. An injunction is a court order that tells the agency or institution to stop a certain activity that has been deemed a violation of the prisoner's rights. This is the most common victory won by prisoners, and is the motivation for most of the changes in correctional policy. The PLRA asserts that the directions given by injunctions must be as specific and unobtrusive as possible. Prisoners may also win damages, which may be punitive, compensatory, or nominal. Punitive damages are large awards that are intended to prevent similar violations of a prisoner's constitutional rights in the future. Compensatory damages are in the form of wages lost or medical bills incurred because of the actions of the defendant. Nominal damages are small amounts awarded to the plaintiff mainly for symbolic purposes.

Agency and the supervisor liability

There are three common situations in which an agency and/or supervisor can be deemed liable for a correction officer's violation of an inmate's civil rights. The first is if there is a failure to supervise, meaning that the supervisor can be proven to have known about a violation of civil rights but to have remained "deliberately indifferent." If a supervisor tacitly condones a violation of the prisoner's rights, he or she can be held accountable. Another situation in which the supervisor or agency may be charged is in a case of failure to train, when the officer is required to perform duties for which he or she should have been trained but has not been. Finally, a supervisor or agency may be held accountable in situations where there is improper supervision, where there have been gross failures in hiring and firing, and when there is ineffective leadership.

In most cases, a state employee who is sued for a tort claim will be defended by the attorney general, and will have his or her costs of litigation indemnified. The scenarios in which the state will defend an employee vary by jurisdiction. As a general rule, however, states are more willing to defend employees for a minor infraction than for a serious criminal infraction.

"Access to courts"

Correctional facilities are required by law to give prisoners some access to legal materials. Because so many inmates are illiterate, institutions must not only provide law books but must offer legal education programs and reading classes. Inmates are also informed about the PLRA, which discourages them from filing frivolous lawsuits.

The different types of "discovery"

In a court setting, discovery is the right of each side to obtain all useful information before the case is tried. There are a few different ways by which this information may be gathered. A deposition is when a lawyer from one side of the case interviews a witness from the other side in the presence of a court reporter. The counsel on one side may also submit a written questionnaire, known as an interrogatory, which the recipient is required to complete under oath. Finally, a person on the other side of the case may be given a chance to admit or deny a statement. If the person does not deny or object to the statement within a certain amount of time, the statement will be admitted into evidence.

Some trial avoidance techniques

There are a few different ways to avoid going to trial. Many trials are avoided though out of court settlements, while others are dismissed before they go to trial. The defendant may file a Motion to Dismiss, otherwise known as a Rule 12 (b)(6) motion, which declares that even if all of the allegations made by the plaintiff are true, the plaintiff's rights have not been violated. Another document that can eliminate the need for a trial is a Summary Judgment, in which both sides agree to the material facts of the case and ask a judge to rule on these facts without trial.

List some good rules for testifying witnesses to follow

When testifying in court, witnesses should dress well, arrive early, and speak clearly. Witnesses should be familiar with their testimony, but should not memorize responses. Witnesses should always answer "yes" or "no" without volunteering extra information. If an incorrect answer is given by mistake, a witness should correct it immediately. Witnesses should never exaggerate, and should not be afraid to plead ignorance. A witness should always be courteous to both attorneys. If the witness is either the plaintiff or defendant, he or she should give his or her attorney time to object after each question. Witnesses should always stop talking when the judge interrupts, and, most importantly, should always tell the truth according to the best of their abilities.

Glossary

Segregation: the isolation of an individual prisoner. Prisoners may be separated from the rest of the prisoner population for three different reasons: for their own protection, for disciplinary reasons, and for basic administrative reasons.

Serious incident: any event involving a resident, employee, or visitor of a corrective facility that necessitates medical attention or threatens the security of the facility

Severe mental disturbance: any condition in which an individual cannot take care of him or herself, or in which the individual becomes a danger to him or herself or others

Shadow board: a special board used in corrective facility shops, on which the shape of every tool is outlined in its proper place on the board, so that it is easy to tell when a tool is missing.

Shakedowns: frequent and random searches of inmates, cells, and common areas; the purpose of a shakedown is to find contraband

Shivs/shanks: makeshift knives crafted out of materials commonly found in a correctional facility; common shiv/shank materials include toothbrushes, kitchen utensils, and shards of metal from lockers, bed frames, and from metal shops

Special diets: any system of nutrition that fulfills a therapeutic, religious, or dietetic purpose

Strip search: the examination of an inmate's naked body, bodily orifices, and clothing; strip searches are performed to detect weapons, contraband, and any other abnormalities

Super max institutions: the correctional facilities that feature the highest level of security. The inmates of a super max institution are housed individually and spend all but one hour of every day in their cell. On the rare occasions that inmates are allowed out of their cells, they are typically strip searched, guarded by multiple officers, and placed in full restraints. Most programs, however, are conducted via correspondence or closed-circuit television without the prisoner leaving the cell. Other programs, in particular religious services, are conducted through the cell door.

Three piece suit: the informal name given to the full set of restraints (handcuffs, leg irons, and waist or belly chain)

Training: any activity that aims to teach the prisoners skills that will improve their job performance. Training may be conducted in person, and may be at a specialized training facility.

Type I facility: a minimum security correctional facility; this type of correctional facility is typically designed to help reintegrate into society those prisoners who are near the end of their term

Type II facility: a type of low security correctional facility in which the primary objective is to meet the labor needs of the institution; the inmates in a Type II facility typically have less than a year and a half (18 months) until their release date

Unit Management: the basic system through which a group of officers or counselors manage a wing or cell block of a prison. In order for the principles of unit management to be applicable, the unit must hold no more than 500 inmates, and ideally will hold less than 150. Also, there must be little turnover within the unit in order for the system to be effective. The officers and counselors assigned to the unit will work with the same unit for a long period of time, and will be given most of the decision-making responsibilities regarding programming and living conditions. All general conditions and regulations will be decided by the facility managers. Unit management is designed to increase contact between staff and inmates, so that strong working relationships can be built.

Unity of command: the principle of organizational hierarchy which asserts that it is most effective when a worker only has to report to one boss

Universal precautions: the essential practices of safety and medical care that aim to reduce the spread of disease

Urine surveillance program: the random but frequent collection of urine samples to check for drug use

Volunteer: any person who donates time to improving the programs and activities in a correctional facility

Warden: the chief executive or administrative officer of a correctional facility; also known as the superintendent

Work release: a system whereby inmates are released from a correctional facility in order to work at a place of business sanctioned by the government

Practice Test

1. Which of the following is most important for preventing riots or other disturbances?
    a. Regularly practicing a well-planned crisis intervention plan
    b. Regular group talks given to inmates by the warden or other authority figures
    c. Consistent enforcement of rules and regulations
    d. Fast and detailed reporting of inmate infractions

2. Are inmates allowed to smoke?
    a. Yes
    b. No
    c. They may smoke in their cells, but not in common areas.
    d. The answer varies by jurisdiction.

3. True or False: It is important for correction officers to become friendly with inmates because it promotes understanding and mutual respect.
    True
    False

4. Which of the following is NOT a valid method of rewarding or punishing inmates?
    a. Solitary confinement
    b. Time off for good behavior
    c. Loss of inmate privileges
    d. Blocking mail from an inmate's attorney

5. While making rounds, you recognize a new inmate as a friend from high school you later lost contact with. You have not seen him in nearly 10 years. What should you do?
    a. Nothing, as this sort of thing happens from time to time
    b. Notify your supervisor
    c. Acknowledge the inmate in some way
    d. Offer to show him how to stay out of trouble

6. What is the most important component of a fire safety plan?
    a. Prevention
    b. Fire drills
    c. Learning how to use fire extinguishers
    d. Knowing where each fire extinguisher is located

7. What should you do in the case of a prisoner who is unconscious and might be having a heart attack?
    a. Call for medical assistance and begin mouth-to-mouth resuscitation
    b. Call for medical assistance, skip mouth-to-mouth resuscitation and give chest compressions at a rate of 50 per minute
    c. Call for medical assistance, skip mouth-to-mouth resuscitation and give chest compressions at a rate of 100 per minute
    d. Inform your supervisor and do nothing until medical assistance arrives

8. A police officer who arrests a person is required to "read him his rights," such as the right to remain silent and the right to an attorney. These rights are commonly referred to as…
    a. Civil rights.
    b. Arrest rights.
    c. Three strike rights.
    d. Miranda rights.

9. An inmate is entitled to have his rights read to him in which of the following situations?
    a. When he is separated from other inmates and questioned about criminal activity.
    b. When an undercover officer is put in his cell posing as a fellow inmate.
    c. Every time his cell is searched for contraband, even if his cellmate is the suspect.
    d. Every morning at first head count.

10. What is the main function of disciplinary actions against inmates?
    a. Teaching the inmate a lesson
    b. Maintaining order in the institution
    c. Establishing a degree of vengeance
    d. Rehabilitation of the inmate

11. Dealing with inmates with which of these conditions would NOT require extra precautions to protect the health of officers and fellow inmates?
    a. Hepatitis C
    b. AIDS
    c. Cancer
    d. Avian flu

12. True or False: An officer may legally refuse to touch a homosexual inmate if he has religious convictions against homosexuality.
    True
    False

13. What is the purpose of a shadow board?
    a. To keep track of officer assignments
    b. To make preventing escape attempts easier
    c. To make noticing missing tools easier
    d. To keep track of the progress of union grievances

14. What is the limit on how many times a month an inmate is allowed to meet with his attorney?
    a. A maximum of five times
    b. A maximum of 10 times
    c. A maximum of once a month
    d. There is no maximum

15. How often should keys, tools and other equipment be inventoried?
    a. Once a week
    b. Once a day
    c. At every shift change
    d. Every two hours

16. When moving a group of inmates, an officer should walk…
    a. Behind the group.
    b. Ahead of the group.
    c. To the side of the group.
    d. In the middle of the group.

17. Which of the following is a sign that trouble might be imminent?
    a. An inmate doesn't eat lunch, saying he's not hungry.
    b. An inmate seems to have gained weight in a day.
    c. An inmate says he's sick and asks to see a doctor.
    d. An inmate requests a different cell mate.

18. You and another officer are overseeing a large number of inmates in the recreation room. Suddenly a loud and angry argument breaks out between some small groups, and then two inmates begin shoving each other. What should you do?
    a. Call for backup
    b. Make a mental note to file a report later
    c. You and the other officer should move in to stop the fighting
    d. Call your supervisor and ask for advice

19. You observe another officer giving an inmate a small object in exchange for money. Neither one is aware that you have seen them. What should you do?
    a. Walk over and ask them what is going on
    b. Report the incident to your supervisor
    c. Request a different assignment in the future
    d. Nothing, because it is probably irrelevant

20. True or False: It is appropriate to fire a warning shot if a group of inmates is attacking an individual inmate.
    True
    False

21. Which of the following could be used as a weapon?
    a. Fork
    b. Knife
    c. Spoon
    d. All of the above

22. Many people believe that punishing criminals harshly reduces crime because the fear of going to jail or prison keeps many people from committing crimes. Which word best describes this effect?
    a. Rehabilitation
    b. Deterrence
    c. Incarceration
    d. Recidivism

23. Which of the following is NOT one of the main purposes of incarcerating criminals?
    a. To show other people that crime does not pay.
    b. To protect the public from criminals.
    c. To teach criminals a better way of life.
    d. To help criminals earn a college degree.

24. Which of the following would constitute reasonable grounds for searching an inmate?
    a. The inmate is serving a sentence for drug smuggling.
    b. The inmate makes rude or obnoxious remarks to an officer.
    c. The inmate appears nervous and is walking oddly.
    d. The inmate is not working hard on his job assignment.

25. True or False: An inmate convicted of sexual crimes against children cannot be forced to attend treatment programs for pedophiles while his case is on appeal.
    True
    False

26. A jail inmate who is currently on trial for murder begs his attorney to allow him to take a polygraph test. His attorney makes the arrangements, and the inmate fails the test miserably. How will this affect his trial?
    a. It will not affect it at all.
    b. The judge will tell the jury to consider the polygraph results.
    c. The judge will end the trial and declare the inmate guilty.
    d. The judge will ask the prosecutor how he or she wants to proceed.

27. At shift change, a key is missing. You should report this to your supervisor…
    a. At next shift change.
    b. At once.
    c. During your next break.
    d. After you have spent at least 30 minutes looking for it.

28. Why was the Prison Litigation Reform Act passed?
    a. To provide inmates with attorneys to file lawsuits against correctional facilities.
    b. To provide funds to train inmates to file their own lawsuits.
    c. To reduce the number of lawsuits filed by inmates.
    d. To create a special court reserved for inmate lawsuits.

29. Which of the following would be unethical behavior for a correction officer?
    a. Reporting late for work due to oversleeping.
    b. Working as much overtime as possible.
    c. Filing a grievance against a supervisor.
    d. Signing off on an incident report that contains inaccuracies.

30. Which of the following is NOT a common complaint of lawsuits against jails and prisons?
    a. The facilities are much too crowded.
    b. The health care is inadequate and a threat to inmates' health.
    c. Each day begins with a prayer over the intercom.
    d. The food served is lacking in quality and nutrition.

31. Which of the following is NOT one of the three most common complaints from families of people who committed suicide while incarcerated?
    a. The institution failed to identify the inmate as a suicide risk.
    b. The institution failed to notify the family of the suicide on a timely basis.
    c. The institution failed to monitor the inmate to prevent the suicide.
    d. The institution failed to respond in time when doing so could have saved the inmate.

32. In most situations it is best for a correction officer to…
    a. Follow official policies and procedures as closely as possible.
    b. Use his best judgment about what to do in each situation.
    c. Consult with fellow officers about what to do when that is an option.
    d. Use his discretion while being guided by official policies and procedures.

33. The most dangerous period for inmate suicide attempts is…
    a. The first week of incarceration.
    b. The first hour of incarceration.
    c. The first 24 hours of incarceration.
    d. The first month of incarceration.

34. True or False: Because of non-discrimination laws, a female inmate has no right to request a female correction officer for a strip search.
    True
    False

35. Which kind of correctional institution is often accused of refusing early release to inmates in order to make more money?
    a. Local jails
    b. Private prisons
    c. State prisons
    d. Federal prisons

36. True or False: Minorities are a higher percentage of the inmate population than of the overall population.
    True
    False

37. There are more men in prisons and jails than there are women. What is the ratio of incarcerated men to incarcerated women?
    a. 23 to 1
    b. 9 to 1
    c. 4 to 1
    d. 15 to 1

38. True or False: Jails and prisons are required by law to have a workforce whose racial demographics match those of the institution's inmate population.
    True
    False

39. Which of the following is NOT a requirement for a successful career as a correction officer?
    a. A commitment to honesty
    b. A commitment to integrity
    c. A commitment to continuous improvement
    d. A commitment to non-violence

40. What is the best schedule for searching cells for contraband?
    a. Once a week at the same day and time
    b. Once a month at the same day and time
    c. Once a month on the same day, but at different times
    d. There should be no set schedule

41. Does a correction officer have to join a union?
    a. It depends on the state in which the officer works.
    b. Yes; every correction officer is required to join a union.
    c. No; no correction officer is required to join a union.
    d. An officer must join a union if he wants to be eligible for early retirement.

42. Under what conditions may a correction officer keep a personal weapon in his or her car while parked in the employee parking lot?
    a. A correction officer should never keep a personal weapon in his or her car in the parking lot.
    b. If he or she has a concealed carry permit.
    c. If he or she has a concealed carry permit and written permission from her supervisor.
    d. If he or she has a concealed carry permit and keeps the weapon in the trunk, unloaded.

43. What happens to the personal property of inmates (watches, wallets, clothes) that is removed from them at intake?
    a. It is cataloged, stored and given back when they are released.
    b. It is auctioned off online and the proceeds are used toward paying court costs.
    c. It is stored until all appeals are exhausted; they get it back if they win their appeal, it is sold to pay court costs if they lose their appeal.
    d. It is given back to them once they are assigned a cell.

44. Which of the following would be considered a medical emergency?
    a. An inmate has the flu.
    b. An inmate has chest pain and numbness in his arm.
    c. An inmate has been hiccupping for three hours straight.
    d. An inmate has vomited.

45. If an inmate escapes, which items below should be included in the information provided to the public to in order to assist them to be on the lookout for him?
    a. Age
    b. Height
    c. Race
    d. All of the above

46. Approximately what percentage of federal prison inmates are in the United States illegally?
    a. Five percent
    b. 30 percent
    c. 15 percent
    d. 10 percent

47. True or False: There are times when a correction officer must devise and impose discipline on an inmate on the spot when they have committed an infraction.
    True
    False

48. Which of the following would constitute sexual harassment?
    a. A supervisor offers to give an officer a good review in exchange for sexual favors.
    b. A female officer continues to tell "dirty jokes" even after a male officer objects.
    c. An officer mounts a picture of a nude centerfold model in the break room.
    d. All of the above.

49. Which of the following is the biggest health hazard for correction officers?
    a. Assaults by inmates
    b. Injuries during riots
    c. Job-related stress
    d. Acquiring AIDS from an inmate

50. Which of the following methods of dealing with job stress should be a last resort?
    a. Prescription drugs
    b. Meditation
    c. Deep breathing
    d. Visualization techniques

Answers and Explanations

1. C: There are many factors that go into maintaining a calm and safe environment in a correctional institution, and one of the most important is that rules and regulations must be consistently enforced. Laxity, favoritism and other forms of inconsistency can lead to anger and resentment and should be avoided at all costs.

2. D: Rules about cigarette smoking and other tobacco use vary by jurisdiction. Until not long ago, virtually all jails and prisons in the United States allowed inmates (and staff) to smoke. Concerns about rising health care costs for both smokers and non-smokers led many states to ban smoking in correctional institutions, starting a few decades ago. More than half of the 50 states currently ban smoking, and that number is expected to keep rising.

3. False: Staff members must NOT become friendly with inmates (or members of their families), but should always strive to maintain a professional distance between themselves and inmates. This is not to suggest that correction workers should not care about the welfare of inmates; they should. However, they should not become friendly with them because doing so can cause substantial conflicts of interest.

4. D: Inmates have a right to communicate with their attorneys, and correctional institutions may not block mail to or from an inmate's lawyer. Doing so would be an unconstitutional form of punishment. The other choices are all valid methods for rewarding or punishing inmates.

5. B: If you come across an inmate you know while working in corrections, you should immediately inform your direct supervisor. This includes close relatives, distant relatives, current friends, friends you have not seen for years, friends you have had a falling out with, former co-workers, and all other past and present acquaintances. The potential for a conflict of interest is high in a situation like this, and failing to notify your supervisor immediately could lead to disciplinary action.

6. A: Fire prevention is the most important aspect of a fire safety program. This is not to downplay the importance of knowing where the fire extinguishers are and how to use them, or the necessity of holding regular fire drills. These are all important. However, the best way of keeping people and property safe from fires is making sure one never starts.

7. A: You should request medical assistance and immediately begin mouth-to-mouth resuscitation. This is the general rule, but there could be times when you might have to ignore the rule if following it might endanger you, another officer, or other inmates.

8. D: Miranda rights are named after a lawsuit, *Miranda vs. Arizona*. Here is the Miranda warning given to arrestees: "You have the right to remain silent. Anything you say or do may be used against you in a court of law. You have the right to consult an attorney before speaking to the police and to have an attorney present during questioning now or in the future. If you cannot afford an attorney, one will be appointed for you before any questioning, if you wish. If you decide to answer any questions now, without an attorney present, you will still have the right to stop answering at any time until you talk to an attorney. Knowing and understanding your rights as I have explained them to you, are you willing to answer my questions without an attorney present?"

9. A: You are not required to read an inmate his rights when you are carrying out the day-to-day activities of a correctional institution, such as head count or cell searches for contraband. Undercover officers posing as inmates are also not required to reveal what they are doing. But if an inmate is separated from the rest of the inmate population and questioned about criminal activity, this is considered an interrogation, and that inmate is entitled to a reading of his rights before it begins.

10. B: The main function of disciplinary action is to maintain order in the institution. It should never be used to exact vengeance or "teach someone a lesson." Also, while disciplinary action is not primarily designed to rehabilitate inmates, such rehabilitation may occur in some inmates as a result of maintaining order.

11. C: Cancer is neither infectious nor contagious. All of the other health conditions listed can possibly be spread to others, so proper precautions must be taken to protect the health of officers and other inmates. Your institution will have detailed policies and procedure for handling such situations.

12. False: There is no such right recognized by a court of law anywhere in the United States. Inmates are entitled to equal treatment no matter their sexual orientation or the religious beliefs of officers or other correction personnel.

13. C: Tools can be used as weapons against officers or other inmates, and can be used to help facilitate an escape attempt. For this reason they are kept on wall boards with an outline of each tool drawn around its storage position. This makes it instantly obvious when a tool goes missing.

14. D: The right to counsel is a fundamental constitutional right, and correctional institutions may not infringe upon it. This does not mean that an inmate can force a jail or prison to allow him to meet with his attorney at 3:00 in the morning, or meet with him every day for hours on end on a regular basis. However, there may be times when an inmate needs to spend a lot of time with his attorney, and institutions cannot have arbitrary policies that interfere, such as a maximum number of meetings per month.

15. C: Each officer is responsible for his keys, tools and equipment issued to him during his shift. In order to keep track of them, they must be accounted for at the beginning and end of every shift. If something is missing, the supervisor must be notified at once. An officer should never falsely sign off on a short count.

16. A: Walking behind a group of inmates is necessary for the safety of the officer, as it prevents surprise attacks. Any officer walking to the side would have limited sight of the entire group, and an officer in front would have zero sight.

17. B: All of the other choices represent what are usually normal everyday events with perfectly reasonable explanations. An inmate may not be getting along with his cell mate, or he may actually be sick, or he may not feel hungry. None of these are cause for concern in and of themselves. But sudden changes in physical appearance, such as noticeable weight gain in a few hours or days, is often a sign that something is very wrong.

18. A: A situation such as this is extremely dangerous, and two officers are not sufficient to get the situation back under control by themselves. There is no time to call for advice; you must get officers in the room immediately before things get even further out of hand, both for your own safety and the safety of the inmates.

19. B: You are a correction officer, not a police officer or a prosecutor, so it is not your place to confront the officer and the inmate; doing so could cause a very bad situation. It is also not your place to ignore the incident and do nothing or to ask for a different assignment. You should report the incident to your immediate supervisor as soon as practically possible.

20. False: Firing a gun is using lethal force, and should only be used in cases where someone is using deadly force against another person, or seems about to, such as when an inmate possesses a gun and threatens to shoot someone with it. Also, you should never use your gun to fire a "warning shot."

21. D: All of the above could be, and have been, used as weapons by inmates and criminals. A spoon used as a weapon can be dangerous, despite how harmless it may seem. A person could be maimed for life or even killed after being attacked with a spoon.

22. B: Rehabilitation is the process of helping inmates turn away from crime and make better choices. Incarceration is just another name for imprisonment. Recidivism refers to a person going back to jail or prison after being released because they return to a life of crime.

23. D: Deterrence is one of the aims of incarceration—when people see others going to prison for a long time, they tend to reconsider committing a crime themselves. Keeping the public safe from criminals is also one of the goals. The third main goal is helping criminals see the error of their ways and learn to live better; this is called rehabilitation. Allowing inmates to earn a college degree can be part of the rehabilitation process, but it is not one of the main goals of incarceration.

24. C: A correction officer must have a valid reason to search an inmate. In other words, there must be something that causes the officer to believe that the inmate is hiding something on his person. An inmate who is nervous and walking oddly certainly falls into this category, as it is likely that he is walking oddly because he is trying to conceal something, and his being nervous is a good sign that he is worried about being caught.

25. True: Treatment programs for pedophiles require the clients to admit that they are sexually attracted to children. Forcing an inmate to attend one while his case is still under appeal is seen as a violation of his rights. Only after his appeals have been exhausted can he be forced to attend.

26. A: It will not change the trial at all. Polygraph results are not admissible in courts, even if the defendant volunteers to take one. His attorney would have no obligation to share the results with the judge, prosecutor, or jury.

27. B: A missing key could allow an inmate or several inmates into an unauthorized area. It must be reported at once.

28. C: Many inmates believe they have received unfair treatment somewhere during the process of their incarceration—they did not get a fair trial, the prison is violating their rights, or some other injustice has befallen them. Others are simply bored and turn to researching and filing lawsuits as a hobby. At any rate, the number of lawsuits by inmates was clogging the courts, and the act was passed in order to address this problem.

29. D: Oversleeping and being late for work should be avoided as much as possible, but it can happen. As long as it was not deliberate or due to gross negligence (staying out all night partying) and the officer does not lie about it, it is not unethical. There is also nothing unethical about working lots of overtime or filing legitimate grievances. But an officer signing a report that he or she knows is not entirely truthful is highly unethical.

30. C: Overcrowding, lack of access to adequate health care, and food of low quality and nutritional value are all common complaints of inmate lawsuits, as well as lawsuits brought by others on behalf of inmates. However, these are far from the only reasons people file lawsuits against correctional institutions.

31. B: While it is not unheard of for relatives to complain that there was a delay in notifying them of an inmate suicide, it is not one of the most common complaints around this subject. The three most common are the other ones listed.

32. A: A correction officer should always follow official policies and procedures to the best of his abilities, at all times, and in every situation. There are very few situations a correction officer will ever encounter that are not covered by official policies and procedures.

33. C: A very high percentage of suicide attempts take place within an inmate's first 24 hours of incarceration. There are a variety of reasons for this—drug and alcohol withdrawal, shock at being incarcerated, and depression over bad life choices, to name a few. This is not to imply that this is the only period when inmates attempt suicide, but only that correction officers should be more vigilant about monitoring the inmate during this period.

34. False: Only female correction officers may conduct a strip search of female inmates. However, according to current court rulings, both male and female officers are allowed to conduct strip searches of male inmates.

35. B: Private prisons are run by corporations in order to make a profit. They charge the government a certain amount of money per day, per inmate. This naturally leads many people to suspect that one of the main reasons private prisons deny an inmate early release is to maintain profits for as long as possible.

36. True: African-Americans are about 14 percent of the American male population, but about 40 percent of the prison population. Hispanics are also overrepresented. In 2010, 43 out of every 1,000 black males were in jail or prison. For Hispanic males, the number was 18 out of every 1,000. For white males, the number was seven for every 1000.

37. B: There are about nine times as many men in jails and prisons as there are women. This ratio is fairly consistent all over the country, and has held steady for many decades.

38. False: There is no law making that a requirement and, if such a law existed, it would probably be ruled unconstitutional.

39. D: A commitment to non-violence is not an acceptable trait in a correction officer. Of course, an officer should avoid engaging in violent behavior as much as possible, and that sometimes means taking a lot of verbal abuse from inmates. But there will be times in most officers' careers that using violence to restrain an inmate or inmates is necessary, so a man with a philosophical commitment to non-violence would have to choose between violating his beliefs or endangering himself and others.

40. D: Routine searches conducted on a regularly scheduled basis remove one of the most important elements of a cell search, which is surprise. Routine searches should be conducted on a randomized basis.

41. A: In some states, correction officers are required to join and pay union dues to the labor union authorized to represent officers. In other states, called "right to work" states, union membership is not required.

42. A: Because of safety concerns, correction officers are not allowed to keep a personal weapon in their car while parked on the grounds of the correctional institution, even if they possess a lawful permit to carry a concealed weapon. This is to eliminate the risk that an escapee or someone else could break into the vehicle and take the weapon.

43. A: Personal property is taken from inmates upon intake and recorded and stored until their release, at which time it is given back to them. In many institutions an inmate may authorize the institution to release their property to a person they choose. If they don't make this choice, their property is held until their release.

44. B: Chest pain and numbness in the arm are two symptoms which could indicate a heart attack and the inmate should get medical help immediately. In the other situations, there is a good chance that the inmate will need to see a doctor in the very near future, but none of them would constitute an emergency situation in and of themselves.

45. D: The public should be given as much information as possible to help them identify an escaped convict, such as gender, race, height, weight, age, scars, tattoos, and any other identifying features. The more information the public has, the more likely it is that someone will be able to identify the escapee.

46. B: Official figures vary somewhat, but most experts say that between 27 and 33 percent of federal prison inmates are in the United States illegally.

47. False: A correction officer has no authority to punish or discipline inmates for any infractions, whether serious or minor. The officer must report the infraction to a supervisor and let the proper authorities decide on a punishment.

48. D: All of the scenarios would be considered sexual harassment. Sexual harassment is much broader than someone making an offer of better treatment in exchange for sexual favors, and includes any unwelcome behavior of a sexual nature. It is best to avoid any hint of sexual behavior or conversation at work.

49. C: The chances of acquiring AIDS from an inmate are very low, as are the chances of being injured during a riot. Being assaulted by an inmate is more likely than these two, but even that does not result in stress when it comes to overall damage to an officer's long-term health. Health experts say that stress that is not dealt with can take years off of a person's life expectancy.

50. A: Generally speaking, it is best to avoid taking drugs unless absolutely necessary. Side effects can be very bad, and the drugs might lead to a lower level of job performance, even if only taken after a shift. Natural remedies should be attempted first. Of course, if your physician prescribes a drug, you should follow his advice, but if there is any chance the drug could affect your work, you should let your supervisor know about the situation.

Made in the USA
Middletown, DE
04 April 2016

30734479R00036